REPAIRING JEFFERSON'S AMERICA

"At a time where the concept of civility and civics in the public arena is dying, Clay Jenkinson's *Repairing Jefferson's America* is a sorely needed addition to our national conversation. To be Jeffersonian is to seek an open, accountable government, active citizen engagement with civility, and an elevation of our civil liberties. Clay's book details how we can strive towards a more perfect union and encapsulates a Jeffersonian vision for how our system of government can remain the world's best hope. *Repairing Jefferson's America* aim is to repair our nation 'one person at a time' and to teach us to be better citizens, wiser public servants, and a more noble America."

—Delegate Jason S. Miyares
Member, Virginia General Assembly

"Clay Jenkinson has been inhabiting the personality of Thomas Jefferson for so long that he thinks and speaks Jeffersonian. Now he has carried that gift into print in a book that, while fully aware of Jefferson's human failures, recovers his idealistic vision for an America that has lost its way."

—Joseph Ellis
Author of *American Dialogue: The Founders and Us*

"The best of the American spirit comes from Thomas Jefferson. Clay Jenkinson has provided a truly welcome invitation for the American people to return to their best selves."

—Deepak Chopra
Author of *Books of Secrets: Unlocking the Hidden Dimensions of Your Life*

"Jenkinson rediscovers the vital and robust Jefferson and restores our trust in boldness, optimism and self-reliance."

—Landon Y. Jones
Author of *William Clark and the Shaping of the West*, Former Editor of *People Magazine*

"Jenkinson invites his readers to think in 'the Jefferson way' about everything from good books and precious friends to fine wines and the duties of citizenship. This is a Jeffersonian profession of faith sure to attract a wide audience and spark sharp debate."

—James P. Ronda
Barnard Professor of Western American Literature, The University of Tulsa

Repairing Jefferson's America

by Clay S. Jenkinson

© Copyright 2020 Clay S. Jenkinson

ISBN 978-1-64663-096-7

Published by

◄ köehlerbooks ™

3705 Shore Drive
Virginia Beach, VA 23455
800–435–4811
www.koehlerbooks.com

REPAIRING JEFFERSON'S AMERICA

CLAY S. JENKINSON

VIRGINIA BEACH
CAPE CHARLES

For Catherine Missouri, who has already exceeded all
of my expectations.
May the American republic recover in time for
you to enjoy the bloom.
Everything I do is for you.

Jean-Antoine Houdon's 1789 bust presents Thomas Jefferson as a serene exemplar of the Enlightenment.

I have lived temperately, eating little animal food, & that, not as an aliment so much as a condiment for the vegetables, which constitute my principal diet. I double however the doctor's glass and a half of wine . . . the ardent wines I cannot drink, nor do I use ardent spirits in any form. Malt liquors & cyder are my table drinks, and my breakfast . . . is of tea & coffee . . .

I am not so regular in my sleep . . . devoting to it from 5 to 8 hours, according [to how much] my company or the book I am reading interests me; and I never go to bed without an hour, or half hour's previous reading of something moral, whereon to ruminate in the intervals of sleep. But whether I retire to bed early or late, I rise with the sun . . .

Table of Contents

Foreword

In the fall of 2005, I received a phone call which I did not expect, and I had no premonitions about how consequential it would be. It was from Clay Jenkinson's office. Clay was moving back to his native state of North Dakota and needed to establish a new home for his public radio show, *The Thomas Jefferson Hour*. The caller asked whether I would consider being a temporary guest host for the program until a permanent one could be found. Intrigued and flattered, I accepted.

So began a fifteen-year friendship with both Thomas Jefferson and Jenkinson, the Jeffersonian scholar who portrays the third US president. I have since become the semi-permanent guest host, which I consider a term of endearment and refuse to relinquish. Most years this means I'm privileged to have fifty-two private conversations—one a week—with Jenkinson/Jefferson. One might think after a decade and a half the subject matter would be exhausted, but the opposite is true. As America grows, changes and faces new challenges, so does Jefferson's influence and perspective.

The Thomas Jefferson Hour includes a podcast that draws listeners from around the globe, and the program is broadcast over seventy public radio stations in twenty-three states. We receive questions from Asia, the Middle East and Europe, and throughout America. People want to know Jefferson's views on gun rights, government, and religion. They ask about Jefferson the polymath and how "all men are created equal" could be professed by an owner of enslaved people.

I sit across from Clay and present these questions and watch as he "becomes" Jefferson. There is a perceptible change in the position of his head, his body language shifts, and I see something different

1

in his eyes. While in character, he is Jefferson, teaching us how to be Jeffersonian, awkward as that may be for him while discussing the behavior and morals of a man from the eighteenth century.

In *Repairing Jefferson's America*, Clay provides a roadmap to help citizens grapple with some of the most difficult issues facing our nation during a time of political polarization and global turmoil. America may have lost its way, Clay suggests, but through Jeffersonian principles we may again find light in the darkness. "You don't have to do everything in this book to be a Jeffersonian," he writes. "Jefferson believed in human freedom, and he certainly did not hold himself up as the epitome of human enlightenment. It would be great if all of us tended vegetable gardens and read Homer in the original Greek, but as John Adams might say, 'We live in the real world.'"

I firmly believe that the real world is what we make it.

It was a lucky phone call.

David Swenson

Introduction

The national awakening to the myriad legacies of slavery and systematic racism have caused all of us to think hard about such historical figures as George Washington, Theodore Roosevelt, and Thomas Jefferson. Jefferson gets the largest percentage of criticism among the Founding Fathers because he was the one who wrote, "We hold these truths to be self-evident, that all men are created equal." If that statement means anything, it has to cover all human beings, male and female, of all races and ethnic groups, of all religious sensibilities, irrespective of wealth, social status, or any other "accident of birth."

We don't know precisely what Jefferson meant when he wrote those words or how widely he expected the proposition to be interpreted in his time and later in American history. What we do know, without doubt, is that Jefferson was a slaveholder, a racist, and an appartheidist. One need only read *Notes on the State of Virginia* and his 26,000 letters carefully to see that while he hoped that the slaves in the United States would be freed—at some point—he could not contemplate a biracial republic with any equanimity. What he wrote about African Americans in *Notes on Virginia* is hard to read in our time, as it was for many enlightened individuals in Jefferson's time.

So, should we pluck down Jefferson statues, demolish or repurpose the Jefferson Memorial in the District of Columbia, and blast his visage off of Mount Rushmore? I hope not, for several reasons.

3

First, I subscribe to the "whole man theory" of historical evaluation, and though Jefferson's record on race and slavery is a significant blot on his character and achievement, it should not be regarded as the only measure of his historical importance. Jefferson made important contributions to American and public architecture, to the Library of Congress and library classification, to the science of paleontology, to our coinage system and the rectangular survey grid system. He wrote the profoundly important Virginia Statute for Religious Freedom. He created, admittedly with slave labor, the University of Virginia, one of the greatest universities in the English-speaking world, and the template for university campuses throughout the New World. Jefferson was a patron of science, literature, political theory, landscape gardening, wine culture, and he set in motion the exploration of the American West, in particular the Lewis & Clark Expedition of 1803–06. Jefferson's creative "footprint" can be seen across the spectrum of American life. While it is true that he could not have achieved what he did without the forced assistance of hundreds of enslaved people, it does us no good to try to erase his place in American history. We must wrestle with his complicities, as we must wrestle with our own.

Second, Jefferson's record on race and slavery is not uniformly bad. He encouraged Congress to abolish the slave trade in 1808 (successfully), and helped to keep slavery out of the old Northwest with his 1784 Plan for the Government of the Western Territory, which influenced the Northwest Ordinance of 1787. Jefferson attempted on several other occasions to persuade his fellow Virginians to abolish slavery either gradually or in one great act of racial justice. He was well-known for his condemnation of slavery. The passages in *Notes on Virginia* that decried slavery were used by abolitionists through the remainder of the nineteenth century to call for racial justice. Don't get me wrong. Jefferson's record on race and slavery is plenty bad. But it is much more nuanced and complicated than we sometimes choose to think.

Third, if we want to understand America, we have to try to understand Jefferson. His inconsistencies, his paradoxes, are the paradoxes of the American experiment. Much better to engage in a continuous national conversation about Jefferson, the Founding Fathers, and the inconsistencies of the American experiment— whose heirs we all are—than to turn away in disgust. I would alter the chiseled paragraphs in the Jefferson Memorial to exhibit that which is not enlightened in Jefferson's writing. Several of the statements are quoted out of context to make him appear more enlightened than he actually was. It would be easier—and more culturally mature—to display the whole truth on those Palladian walls than to present Jefferson as less imperfect than in fact he was. In my view, any assessment of Jefferson's achievement in any area—from the 1,000-foot garden terrace on the south side of Monticello to the Louisiana Purchase to the First Inaugural Address or the University of Virginia—should now include an asterisk noting that he could not have achieved what he did if he were not supported all of his life by the blood and sweat and tears of enslaved men, women, and children.

Fourth, we don't fix America by erasing the things we now find intolerable. We must attempt to be fair, reasoned, deliberate, and contextual in exploring our troubled history. Like it or not, we are the heirs of generations of imperfect men and women. The notion that we have emancipated ourselves wholly from the racism, sexism, imperialism, colonialism, Eurocentrism, and other weaknesses of our national experiment is problematic. We definitely need to think in new, more generous, more inclusive ways about who we are and where we came from, who contributed to our national history, and who should no longer get a "pass" on the most significant questions, as Jefferson did for much of American history. But I constantly try to remind myself of two things. First, as my mentor Everett Albers said, "judgement is easy, understanding is hard." I try to live by that principle. Second, I always wonder "What will they say of us?" and I tremble when I try to contemplate that.

Fifth, for all of his grievous faults, it was Jefferson who found that imperishable language, "We hold these truths to be self-evident, that all men are created equal, that they are endowed by their Creator with certain unalienable Rights, that among these rights are Life, Liberty and the pursuit of Happiness." Judge him as you wish, but we can never live without his ideals. His words not only serve as a rebuke to his own weaknesses and bigotries, but to ours. Even if Jefferson did not fully subscribe to the words that he wrote, or see his own hypocrisies, he formulated a sentence that has fueled liberation movements for 250 years and which constitute the one sentence no free people can ever live without.

I love America. I believe most Americans are idealists, even if they are disillusioned idealists. I see this book as a guide to the perplexed. Most of the people I meet want more from their lives. But they are a little unsure of themselves because the corrosive energies of conformity, consumerism, and philistinism are swirling all around them and sometimes eating them up. In a sense, I hope this book is for every reader a kind of personal Declaration of Independence from the complacent civilizational collapse we see all around us.

I don't want us to give up as an aspirational nation and just settle into a life of vacuous consumerism. I don't know about others, but I don't think either of the two major political parties in America represents my values or my interests. Although both parties claim Jefferson when it suits their purposes, neither party represents truly limited government, fiscal responsibility, self-reliance, science, political harmony, civility, education, and human freedom.

As pointed out, Jefferson was an imperfect embodiment of the Jeffersonian, if that makes any sense, but what he stood for is, in my opinion, what's missing from American life in our time. We need a Jefferson Party (unlikely) or at least a Jeffersonian Movement if we are ever going to recover. Each of us needs to rededicate our life to enlightenment, so that we can in turn insist that America rededicate itself to higher purposes.

I invite people who want more from their country, and more from their individual lives, to read this book and work consciously to become Jeffersonians. Every time I think about Jefferson's life as an amateur architect, amateur scientist, man of letters, scholar and political philosopher, a man who cultivated friendship and pursued the good life with impeccable manners and generosity of spirit, I want to be more like him.

We need to bow to science, argue from evidence, agree to disagree as rational friends, seek consensus, and treat each other as equal *citizens* of a republic, not as tribes, social classes, or ideologues. Jefferson is not the only answer to our problems, but he is one of the best answers. He believed we were up to it, that we could govern ourselves. We need to prove we can really do that. This is a cross between a self-help book (you too can be a Jeffersonian!) and a mirror to hold up to the horror show that is the current state of public life in America.

I am often asked in these troubled times how worried I am about this self-governing experiment called America. The answer: *deeply worried.*

In 2001, G. W. Bush became president by a 5-4 vote of the US Supreme Court along partisan lines. His legitimacy is questioned by some. Eight years later, Barack Obama was widely regarded outside Democratic circles as a crypto-Muslim intruder into America's constitutional system. His legitimacy is questioned by millions, including the man who would be his successor. The Senate majority leader publicly vowed to do everything in his power to make Obama's presidency a failure.

In 2016, Donald Trump won the presidency in an election that the entire US national security apparatus determined was interfered with by Russia. That raises the issue of legitimacy. Trump also lost the popular vote to his Democratic opponent, which in the minds of some raises additional issues about whether he is the legitimate choice of the American people. The president continuously sides with the president of the Russian Federation in questions of Russian interference in the election.

That amounts to a trail of legitimacy issues for the last three elections and the last twenty years.

As I write this, the United States has descended into a divisiveness that threatens to tear apart the very fabric of civility and compromise upon which our government is based. President Trump was impeached in late 2019 by the US House of Representatives, and then acquitted by the US Senate. He was charged with two articles of impeachment. The first charge was for abuse of power in pressuring Ukraine to announce that it was investigating Trump's principal political rival, Joe Biden, and withholding urgently needed military funds until Ukraine complied with that demand. The second charge was for obstruction of Congress in not complying with congressional subpoenas for documents and for administration witnesses to appear before Congress. His acquittal along strict party lines only deepened a cultural chasm that, I fear, is on a par with the crisis we faced in 1860. Carl Bernstein has called what we are facing a "Cold Civil War." I believe he is right. Trump was the fourth president in our nation's history to endure an impeachment challenge. None of them resulted in a sitting president being removed from office. Three of those impeachments came within the past forty-five years, and two within the last twenty-one. The Constitution shows signs of breaking up.

It is my fervent conviction that only through a return to Jeffersonian principles can we transcend the political chaos eroding the foundation of American citizenship and governance. For me, it is this simple.

We must stop attempting to delegitimize our presidential elections. We must return to what the late John McCain called "regular order." We must commit ourselves to a return to mutual respect, honorable opposition, fair play, and a fundamental devotion to a commonweal. The behavior of the most extreme partisans of our culture is pushing us in the direction of the Roman Republic in its final days, just before all order broke down and Pompey, Crassus, Caesar, Brutus, Cassius, and Augustus Caesar addressed Rome's constitutional problems by way of civil war. Are we Rome? Yes and no. So far more *no* than *yes*, but things are slipping away from us fast now.

Beyond this, the partisan paralysis of the US Congress has left us without a national healthcare policy, national energy policy, national immigration policy, or national education policy. Our infrastructure is deteriorating.

Great nations find ways to address their fundamental problems. I'm not wedded to any solution to each of these challenges, but I know they need to be sorted out with science, good sense, compromise, and pragmatism. While we dither and wield Fox/MSNBC brickbats, the other great nations of the world are striding forward into the middle of the twenty-first century. We are in danger of being left behind. In some ways *we have been* left behind.

We hear lots of talk about the robustness of our democracy, but I think it is much more fragile than we think, and I believe there is a real possibility of the collapse of the American republic. The armed gangs have not taken to the streets—yet.

Jefferson More Than Ever

What a stupendous, what an incomprehensible machine is man! who can endure toil, famine, stripes, imprisonment, and death itself in vindication of his own liberty, and the next moment be deaf to all those motives whose power supported him through his trial and inflict on his fellow men a bondage one hour of which is fraught with more misery than ages of that which he rose in rebellion to oppose.
Jefferson to Jean-Nicholas Démeunier, *June 1786*

Thomas Jefferson was America's greatest optimist. From the west portico at Monticello he looked out on the vast interior of the continent and dreamed of a rational agrarian republic with minimal government, a fresh start for enlightened man "with room enough for the thousandth and the thousandth generation." He was thrilled that a 3,000-mile moat separated the American republic from the madness, havoc, and history of the Old World. Jefferson's spirit was in harmony with Thomas Paine, who wrote, "We have it in our power to begin the world over again. A situation, similar to the present, hath not happened since the days of Noah until now"— and with the French agrarian Michel-Guillaume Jean de Crèvecoeur, who asked, in his 1782 *Letters from an American Farmer,* "What then is the American, this new man?" Jefferson believed "this new man" would be the most self-actualized and rational being who ever walked the face of the earth, and that the destiny of America was to produce the first truly enlightened nation in human history.

Jefferson embodied much of that dream. He was America's Renaissance Man. He could, as his early biographer James Parton put it, "calculate an eclipse, survey an estate, tie an artery, plan an edifice, try a cause, break a horse, dance a minuet, and play the violin." He knew seven languages, three ancient and four modern. He was the father of American paleontology, library science, wine culture, and neoclassical public architecture. He wrote more than 25,000 letters with his perfect, even artistic penmanship. Without ever becoming a traditional politician, he served in virtually every major office available to an American citizen of his time (governor of Virginia, Virginia congressman, ambassador to France, secretary of state, vice president, and the third president of the United States). He amassed one of the largest private libraries in the New World, in his view the most carefully chosen library in America. He wrote one of the first American classics, *Notes on the State of Virginia* (1785). He was one of America's greatest gardeners. And he wrote two of the most important documents in the history of human liberty: the Declaration of Independence (1776) and the Virginia Statute for Religious Liberty (passed in 1786). Emerson famously said an institution is "the lengthened shadow of one man." When, in his retirement, Jefferson invented the University of Virginia, he laid down the template for virtually all subsequent American university campuses, what he called his "academical village."

Perhaps most important, Jefferson believed that we were up to the challenge of enlightened self-government. He believed we are capable of being (or becoming) our best selves. In fact, he believed that our republican system of government would only succeed if each of us strove to become our best selves, and maintained that level of self-actualization much, if not all, of the time.

I love America. I'm an optimist. I believe that the vision of the Founding Fathers, particularly Jefferson, offered America the best chance in history to perfect the human project. Unfortunately, the course of human events has made it almost impossible for us to remain a republic. Frederick Jackson Turner (1861–1932) wrote that the 1803 Louisiana Purchase by itself probably necessitated the death of any realistic chance we had of maintaining republican forms and values.

After the Civil War we largely gave the United States over to the robber barons. We thrust ourselves into Cuba and the Philippines in what Secretary of State John Hay called a "splendid little war." Thereafter we were drawn into world domination, in part by the hectic personality of Theodore Roosevelt, more fully during and after our reluctant intervention in the two world wars of the twentieth century. Since 1945 we have been a commercial, political, and military world empire, though a somewhat reluctant and on the whole benign world empire.

Some of these changes were made inevitable by the tragedy of European history and by the sheer size, resource base, and economic enterprise of America.

We are a great nation, but, like the ancient Romans, we ceased to be a republic long before we were willing to admit it, and the tension of trying to pretend to be a republic—still trying to govern ourselves with a republican Constitution when it can no longer be stretched to cover the things a great world power must inevitably do, at the pace it must do them—is one of the principal causes of the political disruptions of our time. More than any other statesman of our history, Jefferson understood that cultures are dynamic, not static—that no constitution, however worthy at ratification, can be expected to have a very long shelf life in an evolving and dynamic society.

Jefferson advocated tearing up the Constitution of the United States once every generation. Instead, we have amended the Constitution merely twenty-seven times, and at least half of those amendments are procedural rather than substantive.

It's impossible to know precisely when the United States ceased to be a republic, but that unfortunate development occurred a very long time ago. Some would draw the line at the ratification of the Fourteenth Amendment (July 9, 1868). Some at the closing of the frontier (1890) or the Spanish-American War (1898). Some choose the geopolitical machinations that led to the American creation of the Panama Canal (1903–14), others America's entry into World War I (April 6, 1917), or August 6, 1945 (Hiroshima). Theodore Roosevelt inaugurated the American Century by arguing that the British Empire was beginning to decline, and since nature abhors a vacuum, the United States needed to take its place in the world arena as a full global power. When Roosevelt sent the Great White Fleet around the world in 1907–09, he was essentially issuing a news release to the world that America had arrived, and nothing would ever be quite the same in the international arena.

I don't wish to blame the People for taking their eyes off the ball and letting our republic slip away. It is more complicated than that. I used to say that we have become a Hamiltonian nation with a thin Jeffersonian veneer. That was when I was convinced that we were still trying, however imperfectly, to maintain some of the principles of a republic. But I believe it is fair to conclude that even Alexander Hamilton would now lament what we have become. Just when I thought things were bad in the American experiment but understandable, and not without a certain nobility and innocence, we started to hurtle towards collapse. We passed over some sort of invisible boundary between 1980 and the year 2000, and became what we now are: an incredibly wealthy, materialist, obese, vulgar, uncivil, smug, ignorant, complacent, and increasingly nationalist empire, better represented now by Costco and Burger King than by the Lincoln Memorial or the Library of Congress. We have slipped from the top tier of measurable indicators—in literacy, numeracy, longevity, infant mortality, poverty rates, health, access to healthcare, access to education, and overall cultural literacy. Not all of us, of course. But I'd say the great majority of the American people have physically, morally, politically, and spiritually *let themselves go.*

It's agribusiness now, the military-industrial-petroleum-cybernetic complex, the Koch brothers, enhanced interrogation and extraordinary rendition, the Kardashians and cat memes.

The will of the mass of Americans is now simple: *"Keep the stuff coming—do whatever you have to do in the world to keep the gas pumps and the Walmarts full, do what you have to do to make the world conform to our will, but please don't tell us much about it. We prefer to live under the illusion that we are a constitutional republic."*

A passage from Salman Rushdie's *Fury* percolates up into my brain every month or six weeks. I always look it up and read it anew and agonize over it. Sometimes I dismiss it as unfair. Other times I have to take a walk because I find its insights, on the whole, so apt, or at least worth factoring into any diagnosis of where we are now:

> *Were all empires so undeserving, or was this one particularly crass? Was nobody in all this bustling endeavor and material plenitude engaged, any longer, on the deep quarry-work of the mind and heart? O Dream-America, was civilization's quest to end in obesity and trivia, at Roy Rogers and Planet Hollywood, in USA Today and on E!; or in million-dollar-game-show greed or fly-on-the-wall voyeurism; or in the eternal confessional booth of Ricki and Oprah and Jerry, whose guests murdered each other after the show; or in a spurt of gross-out dumb-and-dumber comedies designed for young people who sat in darkness howling their ignorance at the silver screen . . . what of the search for the hidden keys that unlock the doors of exaltation? Who demolished the City on the Hill and put in its place a row of electric chairs, those dealers in death's democracy, where everyone, the innocent, the mentally deficient, the guilty, could come to die side by side? Who paved Paradise and put up a parking lot?*

In my view, we are not quite there yet, and we must not let this be our national epitaph.

The good news is that most of the people I meet want more than a Barcalounger, the Super Bowl, Velveeta cheese, and the

Kardashians. This book is for all of you who are disillusioned with America but still hopeful that we can recover. I'm one of them. And if we cannot recover as a nation, at least we can individually and in small clusters seek a more thoughtful, civil, culturally satisfying, rational, and aspirational life.

Is Thomas Jefferson the answer? No. He lived then and this is now. He believed we could be an agrarian republic. That moment has been gone at least since 1917, when the first mass-produced farm tractors were introduced to the heartland. Jefferson believed that women were happiest in the nursery and we should discourage them from wrinkling their foreheads with politics. He believed that slavery would fade away magically and that American Indians would slip over the western horizon without any significant resentment. The problem with Jefferson is that he believed the most significant problems of the American experiment (slavery, Indian relations, class struggles, environmental concerns) would be resolved in some never-quite-articulated magical way, and therefore he did not need to wrestle the central paradoxes of the American republic to the ground.

Jefferson lived in a three-mile-per-hour world. Once, boldly, he speculated that the earth might be as many as 60,000 years old. If Thomas Aquinas had visited Monticello, he would have recognized the agricultural practices as essentially unchanged. Jefferson could not permit himself to embrace the idea of the extinction of species. He never had a ride in something with an internal combustion engine.

The third president is out of touch with the world that he did not live to observe. He is also a serious cultural problem. Just when we need the enlightenment of Thomas Jefferson more than ever before, he is a wounded, even stricken historical figure. Race may not have fully caught up with America, but it has caught up with Jefferson. When I first encountered Jefferson thirty years ago, he was easily the most compelling of the Founding Fathers. He was riding high as the philosopher prince of America. Everyone knew that he was a slaveholder. Few yet were convinced that Sally Hemings was his common law wife. He was almost regarded as an *accidental slaveholder* then, as if he were a passive man of enlightenment who unfortunately happened to have been born into a world of slavery and made the best of it, and would have made it go away if he could have accomplished that desideratum. He was given a pass in most circles.

Now, a couple of decades later, his name is being removed from elementary schools and city streets. His statues at the College of William and Mary and his own University of Virginia are vandalized, and many call for their outright removal as part of the larger de-Stalinization of America. Charlottesville is no longer celebrating Jefferson's birthday. When I started thinking about Jefferson around 1984, people whispered about Sally Hemings in hushed and cautious terms. Back then a visitor to Monticello could not mention the name of Sally Hemings without receiving a polite but firm rebuke from the gracious but defensive docents. Today, serious historians declare that Jefferson raped Sally Hemings for thirty-four years, that he was a predatory pedophile, that his relations with his daughters were psychologically incestuous, that he raised baby slaves for the sale barn, and that he, more than any other single figure, left us a legacy of racism, structural racism, apartheid, crime, and broken black families. At the same time, Jefferson advocated Indian removal policies that barely distinguish him from his successor Andrew Jackson, and there were times, admittedly few, when he fantasized about the extermination of at least some portions of Indian America, if they could not just be banished beyond some magically-receding western terminus of the republic.

By now it is clear that the man Thomas Jefferson was not always equal to the ideals he beautifully, even profoundly, espoused, and I do not wish to be perceived as somehow "in denial" about the dark side of Jefferson's life and character. Some now refuse to listen to Jefferson because they cannot stomach what they perceive as his contemptible hypocrisies. They have stopped listening to Jefferson's Enlightenment pronouncements because they cannot help but deconstruct them in light of Jefferson's sometimes deplorable actual behavior in the world. Some postmodernists believe that the ideals that Jefferson espoused are inherently problematic, even meaningless, just abstract formulations of patriarchal men bent mostly on maintaining their social and political advantage using all the tools at their disposal.

Needless to say, I disagree with much of the current assault on the life, character, and legacy of Thomas Jefferson, particularly its righteousness and its virulence. I'm with the character Prospero in Shakespeare's *The Tempest,* who introduces to his fellow Europeans an indigenous (and barbarous) protégé, acknowledging his colonial perspective but also anticipating Sigmund Freud by saying, "This thing of darkness I acknowledge mine." Two of my favorite verses from the Bible are John 8:7—"He that is without sin among you, let him first cast a stone"—and Matthew 7:3—"Why beholdest thou the mote that is in thy brother's eye, but considerest not the beam that is in thine own eye?"

My great mentor in the humanities, Everett C. Albers, taught, "Judgment is easy, understanding is hard." Our challenge is to try to understand Jefferson, to wrestle with him from within a generous cultural context, to try to determine what formed him and to what extent he challenged the traditions, mores, and prejudices of his formation. We must search for nuance, and we must be alive to the complexity of history. Our challenge is to study Jefferson (and everyone else) unblinkingly, not flinching or letting ourselves get defensive, but with scrupulous and earnest devotion to the whole truth and nothing but the truth, to the extent that we can see that truth "through the glass darkly." And to withhold judgment as long as possible.

The paradox of our time is that just when we urgently need to recommit ourselves to the principles of the Enlightenment and the pursuit and protection of a genuine American republic, the central genius of the American dream is no longer available to us as an uncompromised inspirational historical leader of the revolution.

Nor are the other founders, including the three current favorites, Hamilton, Madison, and John Adams, likely to lift us to our goal. I continue to believe that Jefferson's vision of America, properly translated and contextualized for an era he did not live to see, is our best hope for the future. We need to be Jeffersonians without letting the problem of Jefferson himself trip us up unnecessarily. We need to pursue the best of his program for human liberty and human happiness, and not succumb to the fallacy that he has nothing more to say to us because he was imperfect in some fundamental ways.

What Jefferson wanted more than anything else was severely limited government, administered by modest and reluctant representatives who would rather be home tending their fields. He wanted well-educated, self-sufficient, and eternally vigilant citizens to do whatever it took to protect their liberties and their natural rights. He wanted our leaders and representatives to be high-minded, virtuous (in the Roman sense of the term), selfless, and exceptionally frugal with our tax dollars. He wanted everyone to be treated identically by what he called the machine of the law. He wanted an American republic that turned away from war and glory and profit, and dedicated itself instead to science and the arts, to harmony and to peace. He wanted America to mind its own business while striving to become the world's template of good government, enlightenment, and human happiness.

He envisioned a secular alternative to Jonathan Winthrop's shining city on a hill. Jefferson was one of the fathers of American exceptionalism. He believed we were going to write the software for the second half of human history. To put it in contemporary terms, he believed in soft power, not hard economic and military power. His program found its first great expression in Pericles' Funeral Oration from Thucydides' *History of the Peloponnesian War* (ca. 411 BCE): the best defense for Athens is to be the greatest, most aesthetically compelling, most educated, most enlightened, most just city-state on earth.

Jefferson did not want the United States to be two countries inhabiting the same continent: one for the rich minority, who live above the law and believe themselves entitled to wealth and privilege, the other consisting of the masses who scratch out a living on the other side of the gated communities. He had seen that up close in France on the eve of its cataclysmic revolution. "It is a true picture of that country to which they say we shall pass hereafter," he wrote, "and where we are to see god and his angels in splendor, and crouds of the damned trampled under their feet." Jefferson wanted every American to have a comfortable sufficiency, and he hoped nobody would accumulate obscene amounts of money and property. He wanted government functionaries to be hesitant to take either liberty or money from the American people. He saw government as "a few plain duties performed by a few honest men." He hoped we could be a fourth or fifth-rank nation like China (then) or Canada (today), pursuing the arts of civilization rather than the grubbier and darker goals of national life. He wanted everyone to live close to nature, to grow something, if only a plate of peas or a rutabaga or a peach.

I want to live in that America.

And here we are now, a bloated world empire, a welfare state, undereducated, complacent, self-satisfied; pretending—for the purposes of a quadrennial pageant of mythology—to be a republic or a democracy.

When I was growing up I thought America was "the world's best hope," as Jefferson put it, and I believed that we usually did the right thing in the world or tried to, exemplified lofty ideals, and sought the path of due process, peace, and justice; that we wanted to lift up every American until he or she could enjoy the American dream. I knew we weren't perfect (we were fighting a war in Vietnam, we still tolerated segregation), but I believed that we were still working our way along that long trajectory towards national perfection. We were educating more people than ever before. Title IX forced our public institutions to provide equal access to women. The civil rights bills were grinding down the lingering antebellum pillars of overt and structural racism. Affirmative action was lifting millions onto a level playing field for the exercise of merit. The raft of environmental legislation of the 1960s and 1970s—clean air, clean water, the EPA, the wilderness act—was breathtaking then; such enlightenment seems nearly impossible to conceive today. The federal courts were forcing bigoted and benighted states to honor the equal protection clause of the Fourteenth Amendment. The courts were quietly insisting that we live up to the spirit of our foundational principles, not merely the letter. The judicial system began to enforce Jefferson's wall of separation between church and state.

One could honestly feel then that we were going to reach the goal, and the Jeffersonians, like the master, would be able to say *nunc dimittis* (Luke 2:25–32), our work is done. Then something happened and we fell apart, tribalized ourselves, and the majority of Americans shrugged off the quest for American enlightenment. We stood by while the maldistribution of wealth—by which I mean access to the fruits of life—was fed steroids by public policy, enabled by the labyrinth of our tax code, openly encouraged by all Republican and some Democratic administrations, and somehow justified as an engine of general prosperity and the free market. During this time the term millionaire was replaced by billionaire, and now billionaire doesn't really describe the profoundly super rich who now own America. When Senator X answers his phone, it isn't to take a call from a goat dairy farmer in Broken Bow, Nebraska. It is to take the call of a coal mining executive. And—can you believe it?—that same senator denounces the "Global Climate Hoax" on the floor of the Senate by holding up a snowball.

In the cynical and disillusioned postmodern world, it is kind of a cliché to be worried about one's country. But I am deeply worried about my country. Hamilton understood where we were heading better than Jefferson, but it cannot all be about power and money and oil and empire and privilege, can it? We may not still exemplify the values of an agrarian republic, but if we are America, we must always strive to respect human rights abroad and at home, to treat every citizen identically, irrespective of race, gender, creed, tribe, or orientation. Of all the nations in the world, we need to be the one that shows the most reluctance to use force. We need to be a nation that refuses to be anything less than at or near the top of the charts in literacy, numeracy, science, the arts, infant mortality rates, longevity, access to healthcare. We need to be the nation where we "retire" or impeach all self-serving politicians. We need to be the nation in which the president of the United States is held to the same standard as a citizen chosen at random, and every citizen strives to have the character of the best presidents in American history.

Reading the paragraphs above, most of my friends would shake their heads or laugh sorrowfully and say, "Where've you been? We haven't been that country for more than 150 years, and maybe never." The fact that intelligent, well-intentioned people can now find our founding ideals quaint or naïve or funny is a sign of how severely we have fallen. We aren't going to be that nation ever again, unless there is a global collapse or environmental cataclysm that shatters the existing world system.

And who wants either of those? I spend the majority of my time trying to imagine how we would turn America around, arrest the slow-motion collapse, reinvigorate the humanities, return to civility and respect and self-reliance, bring *Paradise Lost* and *Pride and Prejudice* back into the curriculum. I know no historical example of a nation that let itself go and then found a way to seek national renewal without being prodded by catastrophe.

We failed to be vigilant. We permitted a vicious class system to spring up in America based not on birth but on wealth. Wealth and power now buy our government. Those who try to say this is not so are lying to us and perhaps even to themselves. The rich and powerful are always at the table. The poor are sneered away, and the middle class is usually not welcome anymore. Whatever the surface government of the United States does or pretends to do, very powerful forces behind the government move senators and representatives around like marionettes, and much of what happens in America and among the other global elites has no effective oversight or regulation. None. Even senators and representatives are, on the whole, mythological window dressing above the subterranean arena where the real decisions about the future of the United States and the world are being made. The most powerful individuals and entities on earth are out of control. We no longer even try to get them back under control. We turn to Netflix for relief. And order in.

I'm painting a pretty gloomy picture. America is so rich that the wealthiest 1 percent can own 95 percent of the wealth of the country, but even the crumbs they leave behind are large enough to buy off rebellion. Forget Marie Antoinette's "Let them eat cake." Let them watch widescreen TVs. Let them have plenty of processed food, fuel, and pocket money, and the great mass of people will forget that they have lost their republic. Feed them gladiatorial sports and cheese in a can, reality TV and Meat Lovers' Pizza, fill all screens with alluring actresses, and they will go to sleep in their Barcaloungers. There could be no revolution in a nation of home theaters.

I don't think we are likely to get much better. We may get worse.

I don't see any true revolutionary feeling in America. Grumbling yes, but rebellion and revolution, no. Still, I don't want to give up, and I don't intend to be defeatist. Each of us can, I believe, do three things:

First, we can get into the arena and fight for our republic. You are going to make some enemies, and even your friends are going to roll their eyes or worry a little about you, but you have to go to the city council meetings, the school board, the Iowa caucuses, the town hall forums, the hearing about the wind towers or the waste disposal project. When people of modesty and integrity stand up and speak with controlled passion about republican values, others listen. Burke was right when he said, "The only thing necessary for the triumph of evil is for good men to do nothing."

Second, we can remember. Our educational system is in danger of forgetting the vision and achievement of the founders, in part because many of them were slaveholders, virtually all were white men and men of privilege, and in part because there is nothing very sexy in civics. My grandmother (a farmer) had only a high school education, but she read the essential books of American cultural and civic life, possessed excellent grammar and wrote in clear, complete sentences using the Palmer Method of penmanship. She was no smarter than ten million fifteen-year-olds, and yet we have abandoned a serious educational curriculum for greater adeptness at accessing pop culture.

We must not forget. For all of its problems, the history of America is inspiring. It would be easy to choose ten books that every young American should read (and still could read); those books could not help but create and confirm idealism in virtually every arena of American life. I don't insist on my list, but let there be literary aspiration among the future leaders of the country.

Third, we can form little Jeffersonian enclaves of like-minded individuals who like to read and engage in conversation and argue with civility and grace and generosity of spirit. Jefferson and his Enlightenment friends spoke of the Republic of Letters. Alexis de Tocqueville spoke of "voluntary associations." Today we might call it networking or a virtual community. If all the Jeffersonians in my zip code stood up, there would be fewer than 100 in the club. If all the Jeffersonians in my state stood up, there would be thousands of women and men of similar values and perspectives, avocations and bookishness, curiosity and determination to see the world through evidence, not hunches. I wish I knew them. If all the Jeffersonians in America stood up, there would be perhaps a million, or maybe even five million revolutionary men and women, depending on how strictly you define Jeffersonian. By all means let us find each other electronically and share ideas, cheer each other on, encourage each other to be our best selves, and let the world know that we exist, we matter, and we mean to be heard. It's time for the Jeffersonians to stop being scattered, isolated individuals.

Both George Washington and Benjamin Franklin developed catechisms to improve their character. Jefferson loved lists and grids and taxonomies and charts. Late in life he wrote his own ten commandments, perhaps a little ironically, to share with a boy named in his honor. I see this book as a mirror that each of us should hold up to ourselves, to assess our self-actualizational progress, to clarify and deepen our resolve to be our best selves as often and as continuously as possible. We cannot all be lean, healthy, elegant, exquisitely civil Renaissance men and women overnight. Perhaps never. But we can make steady progress towards our Idea of ourselves.

The key is to determine the characteristics of a Jeffersonian. That is the purpose of this book. And then to work in our daily lives to adopt those Jeffersonian values that work for us and try to conform to them. That, too, is the purpose of this book.

I meet Jeffersonians in my travels. I am always delighted when I meet a doctor who is also a maker of guitars and ukuleles, a rancher who reads voraciously and wants to talk about the world and life and books, a young intellectual who wants to climb mountains and learn languages, see the world and master chess, float the Grand Canyon, and paint some of its landmarks. America is the home of hundreds of thousands, even millions, of remarkable people doing creative and amazing things. But they either know each other in small, often invisible, clusters, or find themselves swallowed up like a master violinist in Row RR24 at a major league football game. My friends the Jeffersonians say, "Well, even though it's all gone to ruin, I've got a good life. We can travel. We have excellent friends. We read. We'll tend our gardens, and feel a little superior, but probably there's not much we can do about it. It's enough."

It's not enough and you know it. But it's a start.

Time for a new Jeffersonian movement in America. Time for a Jefferson party, or a party with Jeffersonian values by some less controversial name. Time to stand up and be counted. Time to exhibit articulate and evidence-based discourse in the public square. Time to shut off the television and read more books. Time to host some whimsical dinner parties. Time to reach out to every other like-minded individual and encourage their creative energies.

Forget Jefferson. Let's be a *Jeffersonian* nation.

Some of the text that follows was first published in 2004. The materials have been reorganized and slightly modified to more closely reflect our current state of affairs as our constitutional order disintegrates in real time. At this writing, I fear what Margaret Bayard Smith called "this our happy republic" faces the worst constitutional crisis since 1860, as we face seemingly intractable problems and lurch from one contested election to the next.

In writing this book, I have no delusions of grandeur or fantasy that it will have profound influence. But I do believe that the first steps towards national renewal must take place soon or we will be beyond redemption. And even if such conversations do not change the course of human events, they certainly will change individual lives. This book is designed to inspire my fellow citizens to become Jeffersonians and to help create a new Jeffersonianism in America. It is my conviction that everyone who leads a more Jeffersonian life will be more fulfilled, happier, more productive, and more influential. I also believe that people who become Jeffersonians because they wish to live well turn out—as if by magic—to be the natural leaders in all the walks of their lives. We seek the Jeffersonian persuasion in our private pursuit of happiness, but it has important and wholly positive social ramifications. In short, I have attempted here to explore what a Jeffersonian outlook might be at the beginning of the twenty-first century.

Those who are looking for a balanced assessment of Jefferson's strengths and weaknesses will not find it here. I have written about these questions elsewhere. This book emphasizes Jefferson's idealism, his republicanism, his commitment to reason and good sense, and his life as a Renaissance man and an exemplar of the Enlightenment. In other words, this book emphasizes Jefferson's positive vision for the American republic. I believe that the United States needs a new infusion of what might be called clarified (or updated) Jeffersonianism. At the very least, we need to develop a new generation of Jeffersonians, men and women more committed to enlightenment than to mass consumerism.

This book is my modest attempt to define and inspire that national conversation. I have written this book for a broad public, not academic, audience. I have tried to keep the chapters short and the argument clear, so that my suggestions can be read piecemeal, in short bursts, or in one short evening.

The last section of *Repairing Jefferson's America* is an anthology of thirteen Jefferson letters (a baker's dozen). After an agonizing review of my 100 or so favorite Jefferson letters, I have chosen a handful that illuminate the themes of this book, and provide a window into the character and outlook of Jefferson. He was one of the great letter writers of the English language. No two Jefferson scholars would make the same selections. These are letters that have special meaning for me, letters I think every student of Jefferson should come to terms with, letters that help us understand the agrarian republic he was trying to create on the *tabula rasa* of the New World. I've provided brief introductory commentary for each of my selections.

Except in the thirteen letters, I have preserved Jefferson's sometimes idiosyncratic spelling and punctuation in my quotations from his eighty volumes of writings, but I have chosen to capitalize the first word of his sentences.

Citizenship

If once the people become inattentive to the public affairs, you and I, Congress and Assemblies, Judges and Governors, shall all become wolves. It seems to be the law of our general nature, in spite of individual exceptions; and experience declares that man is the only animal which devours his own kind.

Jefferson to Edward Carrington, *January 16, 1787*

If you always lean on your master, you will never be able to proceed without him. It is a part of the American character to consider nothing as desperate; to surmount every difficulty by resolution and contrivance. In Europe there are shops for every want; its inhabitants, therefore, have no idea that their wants can be supplied otherwise. Remote from all other aid, we are obliged to invent and to execute; to find means within ourselves, and not to lean on others.

Jefferson to Martha (Patsy) Jefferson, Aix en Provence, *March 28, 1787*

A **Jeffersonian** believes that citizenship requires much more than occasional voting. Jefferson envisioned active rather than apathetic citizens, and he would be appalled by our propensity to define an American as a consumer rather than a civic individual. Jefferson would surely argue that the American people have no just cause to grumble when they freely abdicate so much of their sovereignty to politicians who pay so little real attention to their interests. Given our infrastructure of citizenship (C-SPAN, email, social media, the internet, public broadcasting, talk shows), Jefferson would argue that there has never been a time in world history when the average citizen was in a better position to participate in self-government and influence the course of events at so little cost.

A Jeffersonian has no choice but to take part in civic life, no matter how time-consuming, frustrating, or enervating it becomes. The Jeffersonian is the sole voice of reason on the local school board.

Jefferson was firmly convinced that we could remain a republic only if we exhibit eternal vigilance and force the commonwealth's formal structures to exhibit unending respect for the dignities and the will of the people. To behave passively towards government is to abdicate the idea of self-government and to give tacit approval to the independent sovereignty and validity of government.

Jefferson intended government to be a genuine expression of the will of the people, not a permanent institution that has its own dynamics, which can exist apart from a continual supply of support from the people. In a sense, Jefferson's government is an entity that can be kept aloft only if the people (not everyone all of the time, but each one some of the time) raise their arms to support it. The minute a substantial percentage of the population turns away to private pursuits, the government falls, because it no longer rests upon the actual strength of the people.

For Jefferson, self-government really means *self*-government, not some tepid brand of citizenship that involves national service only if conscripted, taxation by way of silent withholdings, reluctant jury duty, voting every fourth, or possibly second year, and purely verbal protest on those few occasions when one's ox has apparently been gored. The passivity of this would not offend Jefferson, but it would require him to conclude that such minimalist participation in the democratic process does not constitute citizenship, that it precludes the idea of a republic, and that it will almost certainly lead to tyranny.

Jefferson actually believed that over the course of time we would come to govern ourselves directly—that is, that each individual would internalize the ideals of the commonwealth and become a fully self-restraining human being, and that what formal government there was would be extremely small and modest in its scope. In the meantime, each citizen would be a jealous protector of her or his liberty, would bristle at any evidence of governmental self-aggrandizement, and would be prepared to withdraw support from government any time it exhibited a pattern of neglect, abuse, or unauthorized growth.

Jeffersonians believe that protest is one of the most important tools of citizenship and that a republic embraces rather than dismisses its discontented individuals.

A Jeffersonian believes in self-reliance. We may not be able to subsist outside of Hamiltonian institutions any longer, but every Jeffersonian American is aware of how morally and politically compromising it is to be so dependent on transnational corporations, foreign resources, and centralized government for our daily survival. Good Jeffersonians understand their technical, political, and moral relationship to the grids that deliver their food, shelter, electricity, fuel, clothing, and gadgets. An understanding of the supply lines of our civilization is in itself liberating because knowledge is always preferable to ignorance, and an understanding of the ways systems work at least invites the possibility of action (and liberation) rather than passivity.

A Jeffersonian resists the dependencies of modern life, at least in some symbolic way. Jeffersonians grow something, raise some of their own food perhaps, if only a few tomatoes or pears; plant flowers in a window box; nurture a few vines and perhaps press a few grapes. Jefferson was certain that placing one's hands in the earth was one of the keys to humility and human happiness.

Perhaps we cannot, like Jefferson, dance the minuet, read Homer and Plutarch in the original Greek, design a Palladian villa, invent a revolutionary plow, or write a state paper of global importance, but a Jeffersonian attempts to cultivate a range of practical life skills that signify the will to achieve independence.

A Jeffersonian takes pride in knowing how to do things: weld, perhaps, or plumb, bind books, fire a kiln, change the oil, build a desk, sew, quilt, make jelly, design a website, or perhaps build a telescope.

In the face of the dependencies and structural degradations of modern life, these are, of course, merely symbolic declarations of independence, but the Jeffersonian undertakes them because each gesture of independence invites the next, and each tends to build confidence in the proposition that we become more completely human to the extent that we replace a money economy with one based upon competence and gumption. Moreover, every Jeffersonian act we perform serves as a model and perhaps an inspiration to those around us.

The great Jeffersonians get off the grid to the extent possible without becoming silly or primitive. There are Jeffersonians who produce their own water and power supplies, who build their own houses, and who live with minimal contact with the internal combustion engine and its vast enabling infrastructure. These last free men and women are to be admired if not actually imitated because, in Jefferson's words, they "keep alive that sacred fire which otherwise might disappear from the earth."[1]

---

1   *Notes on the State of Virginia*

Rebellion

They were written [notes on the corruption of British judges] at a time of life when I was bold in the pursuit of knowledge, never fearing to follow truth and reason to whatever results they led, and bearding every authority which stood in their way. This must be the apology, if you find the conclusions bolder than historical facts and principles will warrant.

Jefferson to Thomas Cooper, February 10, 1814

It can never be too often repeated, that the time for fixing every essential right on a legal basis is while our rulers are honest, and ourselves united. From the conclusion of this war we shall be going downhill. It will not then be necessary to resort every moment to the people for support. They will be forgotten, therefore, and their rights disregarded. They will forget them-selves, but in the sole faculty of making money, and will never think of uniting to effect a due respect for their rights. The shackles, therefore, which shall not be knocked off at the conclusion of this war, will remain on us long, will be made heavier and heavier, till our rights shall revive or expire in a convulsion.

Jefferson, Notes on the State of Virginia, 1785

A **Jeffersonian** believes that a great people must reconstitute, redefine, refashion, and rethink itself from time to time, at least once per generation. In a famous letter to James

Madison, dated September 6, 1789, Jefferson suggested that the American people tear up their constitution every nineteen or so years. Madison was, to say the least, not convinced, but that did not deter Jefferson, who advocated a literalist adherence to the principle of the consent of the governed. The "earth belongs to the living," Jefferson declared to Madison, meaning that the systems, constitutions, institutions, and protocols of one generation are not automatically appropriate for the next one, and that even where they are appropriate, the unborn ought not to be imposed on by those who have passed from the scene. The new generation may choose to reaffirm the existing constitutional system, but they should not passively inherit it. Each generation must explicitly ratify its constitutional arrangement.

The more cautious Madison replied that continuity, order, and human reverence for tradition are too valuable to jeopardize with whimsical social experiments, even assuming Jefferson was abstractly right about the rights of most of the living generation. Madison found order comforting, while Jefferson realized that it can be a claustrophobic, even a quietly despotic, force in human affairs.

Jefferson was not afraid of change, and he did not believe that the way things happen to be is necessarily the way they ought to be. More importantly, he did not believe things were as they were because they had developed in an inevitable way. He understood that, natural rights aside, most social structures are in fact artificial constructs that bear no special resonance to nature or the fundamentals of existence. "We might as well require a man to wear still the coat which fitted him when a boy, as civilized society to remain ever under the regimen of their barbarous ancestors," Jefferson wrote to Samuel Kercheval in 1816.

Jefferson believed that some issues are so fundamental that they cannot be resolved by routine legislation. This is particularly the case when reforms are requested from holders of power who might stand to lose from a change in the status quo (term limits, redistricting).

Jefferson understood that this is the great advantage of the revolutionary moment. When the social compact has broken down and people have returned to a state of nature, they have it in their power to refashion the world without having to struggle against the massive inertia of existing institutions. Things that exhibit hidebound tenacity within the existing order and seem too deeply rooted to be altered, turn out to collapse without great drama once their artificial aura of legitimacy has been shattered. From time to time a culture needs to return to a State of Nature, to the true anarchic sovereignty of the people, so that the people can reconstitute themselves without unnecessary influence from what Hamilton called "the wise, the rich, and the wellborn."

Jefferson's unstated motto was that there is nothing magical in the way things are. He believed that he stood at the dawn of a new era in which every institution, every habit, every system, every cultural code, every belief, and every received truth would be examined according to the dictates of reason and good sense, and its capacity to promote human dignity and happiness.

A Jeffersonian believes in rebellion, as peaceful as possible, and as bloody as necessary. In other words, a Jeffersonian is aware that some problems never get solved through routine legislation.

Throughout his lifetime Jefferson shocked his contemporaries by his statements endorsing armed rebellion, defending the validity of the French Revolution, including the Reign of Terror, and his general belief that societies need to be rocked by rebellion now and then to keep them from forgetting to serve the rights and happiness of humankind.

So far as we know, Jefferson never struck another human being in the whole course of his life. He was a harmony obsessive who shrank from controversy and everything sordid, rough, and uncivil in life. In other words, he was not a man of violence, and he invariably preferred the smooth path rather than confrontation or struggle. But he knew that terror is an essential tool in the quest for human liberty, and he rightly predicted that "rivers of blood may yet flow between them [the tyrannized peoples of the earth] and their object."

Jeffersonians are profoundly committed to peace and harmony, are not fond of bloodshed in any of its forms, but are careful not to condemn acts of terror out of hand. Jeffersonians keep in mind two things: first, that most terrorists do not delight in mayhem, but turn to it only as the "last melancholy resort" after all peaceful and "legitimate" attempts to call attention to injustice have been exhausted; second, that terror does work—that it has the capacity to call the world's attention to issues that would otherwise be ignored ad infinitum.

For Jeffersonians, the greatest crime against happiness is learning to live with corruption, institutional indifference, and injustice merely because one is afraid, in Hamlet's words, to "take arms against a sea of troubles and by opposing end them." Those who renounce the use of violence in advance condemn themselves to degradation and enslavement, because established powers are unwilling to commit themselves to the same restrained code of engagement, and they count upon the general peacefulness and passivity of their populations in order to dominate them.

A Jeffersonian world is somewhat disorderly, because the people are tearing up their constitution from time to time and surging into the public square with their pitchforks every time government exhibits the habits of tyranny. In a letter to his closest confidant, James Madison, Jefferson cited the Latin maxim, *Malo periculosam libertatem quam quietem servitutem* [I prefer a dangerous liberty to quiet servitude].[2] Jefferson alone of the Founding Fathers was an apologist for rebellion, revolution, even the French Reign of Terror. He was fond of organic metaphors that likened violent revolution to the routine events of the garden. Most famously, he wrote, "The

---

2   To James Madison, January 30, 1787

tree of liberty must be refreshed, from time to time, with the blood of patriots and tyrants. It is its natural manure."[3] It would be difficult to sound more serene about the possibility of mayhem in the streets. This kind of talk led John Adams to ask, "What think you of terrorism, Mr. Jefferson?"

Jefferson cheerfully accepted that liberty is a messy business, that a volatile public, a certain amount of chaos, and even some tyranny of the majority are important (if somewhat inconvenient) signs of the health of a republic. When most of the national establishment was alarmed and offended by Shays' Rebellion in western Massachusetts, Jefferson blithely asked his friend William Stephens Smith, "What signify a few lives lost in a century or two? . . . God forbid we should ever be 20 years without such a rebellion. What country can preserve it's [sic] liberties if their rulers are not warned from time to time that their people preserve the spirit of resistance?" And when the French Revolution descended into its bloodiest phase, Jefferson refused to denounce the Terror. To his protégé William Short he declared, "The liberty of the whole earth was depending on the issue of the contest [the French Revolution], and was ever such a prize won with so little innocent blood? . . . rather than it should have failed, I would have seen half the earth desolated. Were there but an Adam and an Eve left in every country, and left free, it would be better than it now is."[4]

Fair enough, but it must also be acknowledged that there have been great breakthroughs in nonviolent revolution since Jefferson's death in 1826: Thoreau's crabby New England brand of civil disobedience, Mahatma Gandhi's Salt March and hunger strikes, Martin Luther King's nonviolent protests against American apartheid. Had Jefferson been alive to witness these extraordinary moments in the quest for human equality and dignity, he might have been less willing to see blood as the manure of the tree of human liberty.

---

3   To William S. Smith, November 13, 1787
4   To William Short, January 3, 1793

Jefferson believed that government must be kept on the defensive at all times—that the people not only have a natural right to withdraw consent from their social compact, but that they should shake up government from time to time just to remind their governors that they serve at the pleasure of the people and not otherwise. In other words, for the Jeffersonians, liberty is the quintessence of life, and government is a necessary evil.

A Jeffersonian should never be more afraid than when government offers to provide increased security by way of increased authority. He surely approved of the adage sometimes attributed to Benjamin Franklin: "They that can give up essential liberty to obtain a little temporary safety deserve neither liberty nor safety." Jefferson's attitude would be that national survival and national security are the highest good, of course, but that they must be preserved with the profoundest respect for the Bill of Rights, constitutional legitimacy, and the natural law principle that government should intrude upon our liberties as minimally and as humbly as possible. The Jeffersonian's attitude towards the security state is "prove it." "Prove to me that my well-being depends upon my yielding more of my liberty to the state. Prove to me that there is no less onerous way to survive."

Jefferson was aware that government almost never relinquishes powers it has, once gained. He was willing to live in a more volatile, more dangerous, more chaotic world if he could remain free, rather than to seek security and order at the cost of his independence and the panoply of his freedoms. The Jeffersonian must insist that any security measure be candidly explained to the American people, that it be robustly debated, that it be subject to the most unrelenting court review, that dissent be cherished, that any such emergency measure be temporary, and that the government that undertakes it exhibit profound reluctance rather than zeal and satisfaction in the face of such increased authority.

The twenty-first century opens with unprecedented anxiety about the future of the Enlightenment's legacy of freedom. The cheapening and democratization of violence and terror have led millions of otherwise rational people to want their governments to do whatever it will take to provide for their basic security and standard of living. Such people would prefer not to relinquish any of their freedoms—just the opposite—but given the choice between maintenance of their access to security and the fruits of life on the one hand, and the enjoyment of the full complement of their liberties in a rather more dangerous world on the other, they quietly vote for their material rather than their spiritual well-being.

Tyrants and Hobbesians always offer security at the cost of your liberty.

The plain truth is that it is not at all clear that the principles of the Enlightenment can survive in a world where the technologies of terror are more widely and inexpensively accessible than at any previous time in human history, and when one act of spasmodic violence can shatter the lives not merely of a handful of citizens, but of hundreds of thousands or millions of people. The twenty-first century will call the bluff of the principles of the Enlightenment in ways that would astonish Voltaire, Condorcet, Rousseau, or Thomas Jefferson. All those universalist statements about human aspiration voiced by the great minds of the eighteenth century may turn out to have been contingent on a certain technological, demographic, and geographic moment in human history. In a world of cyber-war and cyber-terror, with ICBM missiles that can travel at ten times the speed of sound and explosives that can be hidden in the battery of a laptop computer, the confident universals of the Enlightenment may be shaken, or destroyed. That would be a tragedy for Western civilization, but it cannot be ruled out.

Even so, the Jeffersonians will not succumb to pessimism, and they will resist loudly—but with unclouded eyes—the siren song of security, order, and the status quo.

Government

It would be a dangerous delusion were a confidence in the man of our choice to silence our fears for the safety of our rights: that confidence is everywhere the parent of despotism—free government is founded in jealousy, and not in confidence; it is jealousy and not confidence which prescribes limited constitutions, to bind down those whom we are obliged to trust with power. . . . In questions of power, then, let no more be heard of confidence in man, but bind him down from mischief by the chains of the Constitution.

Jefferson, Kentucky Resolutions, *October 1798*

With all these blessings, what more is necessary to make us a happy and prosperous people? Still one thing more, fellow-citizens—a wise and frugal government which shall restrain men from injuring one another, which shall leave them otherwise free to regulate their own pursuits of industry and improvement, and shall not take from the mouth of labor the bread it has earned. This is the sum of good government, and this is necessary to close the circle of our felicities.

Jefferson, First Inaugural Address, *March 4, 1801*

A **Jeffersonian** believes that government exists solely to fulfill the will of the people, that we need less rather than more of it, that citizens need to be eternally vigilant if they wish to retain their liberties, and that good citizens flare up whenever they sense that government is failing to represent their interests.

Jeffersonians are suspicious of government in general and they assume that any particular government is probably up to no good. A Jeffersonian is a prickly, and at times a crabby, citizen. Government officials are not seen as remarkable beings deserving of special respect, and certainly not majestic in any way, but rather servants of the people who need to be reminded with some frequency that they exist merely to perform tasks on behalf of their sovereign masters, the people. Any pretension to regal status, any expression of arrogance or gubernatorial independence, is swiftly and severely punished.

Jefferson did not see government as a purveyor of blessings. He would have been appalled by the welfare state, first because it necessitates big government and presumes that a central government can ascertain what a large, diverse, and geographically dispersed population needs, and second because it undermines the self-reliance of the citizenry and encourages individuals to abdicate responsibility while looking instead to government for their well-being.

In Jefferson's formulation, citizens are entitled under natural law, if they wish, to govern themselves directly in genuine democracy— every citizen gathering periodically in the agora or public square. Because direct democracy is inconvenient, especially over long distances and for large populations, citizens agree to engage public agents, called representatives, to do their bidding in the public square. These representatives are like proxy agents at a public auction. They do not have the authority to make wholly independent decisions. They do the bidding of their citizens in a faithful, even literalist, way, and on those few occasions when they deviate from what Jefferson called "the decided choice" of their constituents, they candidly volunteer the truth about their actions, without attempting to evade responsibility, and they invite the citizens to retire them to private life if they are offended by decisions made without their direct authorization. When Jefferson purchased the Louisiana Territory in 1803 contrary to his own constitutional theory, he noted that he had done what a guardian might do for his ward, and that the ward (the American public) was entitled to repudiate the actions of the guardian, in which case the guardian "must get out of the scrape as I can."[5]

This was Jefferson's understanding of the principle of self-government and the will of the people. In practice he was inevitably more flexible, especially when he and his Republican friends were in power. The "logic" of this increased confidence was that he believed that he and his friends were in tune with the people in a way that the arrogant Federalists could never be.

People who call themselves Jeffersonians today are much less literal about representation and the will of the people. They are more concerned with the general tenor of government activity, and they routinely entrust their representatives with more freedom of action than would have satisfied Jefferson, in or out of power. There is widespread acceptance nowadays of the idea that average citizens cannot be expected to keep up with all the workings of government and the complex world it represents, and that the will of the people is a general will, not a bill of particulars. Jefferson would have understood this, given the size and complexity of our social fabric, but he would not have liked it. Government in the twenty-first century is inevitably more detached from the will of the people than it was in Jefferson's time, or in his constitutional theory. Perhaps all that can now be expected of a Jeffersonian is that she or he remember that government is intended to be tethered in some dynamic way to the will of the people—that government is not a management team given broad powers to make the corporation prosper.

A Jeffersonian believes in minimal government. In his own time, Jefferson advocated a tiny, almost nonexistent national government (he actually called it the "foreign department"); somewhat more energetic state governments; and still more emphatic local governments, his cherished Anglo-Saxon "hundreds" or "ward

---

5   To John Breckenridge, August 12, 1803

republics." He believed the national government's portfolio should be strictly limited to the powers enumerated in the 1787 Constitution of the United States and that the national government should do only those things that were truly national or international in scope. At the same time, he believed that government, at any level, should do only those things that government alone can accomplish, and that everything else should be undertaken by individual and private enterprise. The goal of the national government, Jefferson wrote, consists of a few plain duties to be performed by a few honest men. He believed that ambition and careerism were the death of republican liberty. In theory, at least, Jefferson declared himself to be a semi-anarchist.

Obviously, a strictly libertarian government is no longer feasible today, given the urban, industrial, electronic, military, and chemical complexities of our civilization. Some people who think of themselves as "Jeffersonians" argue for a libertarian system, but this is to pretend that the world of the early twenty-first century is not fundamentally different from the world of 1803. A true Jeffersonian envisions a government as limited as possible, but as energetic as necessary to accomplish those things that a government must do on our behalf. In other words, a Jeffersonian is an advocate of governmental restraint, not minimalism, and a champion of volunteerism and individual initiative.

Jefferson advocated minimal government chiefly because he had faith in the individual's ability to craft a life for him or herself, and partly because he understood that "the tendency of things is for liberty to yield, and government to gain ground."[6] Although he was no Leninist, Jefferson looked forward to a time when formal government would almost disappear altogether, and highly evolved individuals would govern themselves in the profoundest sense of the term. Such dreams as this led Alexander Hamilton to dismiss Jefferson as an

---

6   Thomas Jefferson to Edward Carrington, 27 May 1788

"intellectual voluptuary," and John Adams to ask whether Jefferson was not perhaps "fast asleep in philosophical tranquility."

Jefferson believed that the history of the world was the story of all the ways in which too much government had spoiled the happiness of peoples and trampled on their rights. Jefferson understood that an upright and well-meaning government was seductively appealing, and that intelligent citizens delude themselves into believing that a government that begins in virtue will never lose sight of its foundational values. Good citizens must force themselves to resist the siren song of the welfare state, because big government soon begins to take citizens for granted, and a government large enough to distribute benefits can just as easily take them away when that becomes more convenient.

Jefferson's governmental minimalism is a source of genuine frustration for modern Jeffersonians—for two reasons. First, Jeffersonians have come to be very fond of certain government programs, knowing full well that the Sage of Monticello would have regarded them with suspicion. The Jefferson who told his close friend Charles Willson Peale that he could not support a national museum, however desirable, without an enabling amendment to the US Constitution, would undoubtedly frown on federally funded public television and public radio, the national endowments for the arts and humanities, the national galleries, perhaps even the Smithsonian and the National Science Foundation. All Jeffersonians prize such agencies. Jefferson would probably have found them disturbing, unless authorized by constitutional amendments, no matter how much he enjoyed or contributed to their programs.

Second, most Jeffersonians are now convinced that the national government is more enlightened than the states and individual communities, and they look to the national government to deliver Jeffersonian goods by, well, Hamiltonian means (big and expensive government programs, and central authority and initiative). They see government as a tool of justice and social progress, and they tend to find Jefferson's minimalism both quaint and embarrassing.

It is at least possible that even Jefferson, had he seen the complexities of the world in which we find ourselves, might have come to terms with a stronger and more proactive national government. But it is not a good idea to assume that he could have made such a revolutionary adjustment in his core political philosophy or that he would be as tolerant of Hamiltonian nationalism as his well-meaning heirs tend to be. The most faithful Jeffersonian attitude would seem to be a consistently skeptical approach to any program, legislation, or initiative that requires a permanent infusion of tax revenue, or swells the scope, depth, energy, or dignity of government. The Jeffersonian perennially asks, "However useful, convenient, or appealing this government function may appear to be, do we truly need it, and is there not some private—or at least more local—way to accomplish the same thing?"

Foreign Relations

I am for relying, for internal defence, on our militia solely, till actual invasion, and for such a naval force only as may protect our coasts and harbors from such depredations as we have experienced; and not for a standing army in time of peace, which may overawe the public sentiment; nor for a navy, which, by its own expenses and the eternal wars in which it will implicate us, will grind us with public burthens, and sink us under them. I am for free commerce with all nations; political connection with none; and little or no diplomatic establishment. And I am not for linking ourselves by new treaties with the quarrels of Europe; entering that field of slaughter to preserve their balance, or joining in the confederacy of kings to war against the principles of liberty.
Jefferson to Elbridge Gerry, *January 26, 1799*

A **Jeffersonian** has a very modest idea of America's place in the world. As the twenty-first century begins, and in the wake of the September 11, 2001, catastrophes, the United States cannot permit itself to want to be isolationist any longer, but we can still honor Jefferson's principle that our best export is the Idea of America: that we should mind our own business as much as possible; build a nation just, equal, beautiful, and culturally remarkable; and then quietly invite the rest of the world to become enamored of our model and our success. Jefferson believed that the United States has no duty or right to police the world. In fact, he believed that entangling alliances with the nations of the Old World could only sully the purity of the republican experiment in America.

Jefferson understood that each country has its own history, tradition, and social dynamic, and that it would be naïve and arrogant to believe that American-style democracy can be transferred intact from the United States to other nations. Asked by Lafayette and others to advise the French people in the midst of their great revolution (1789–1799), Jefferson surprised (and disappointed) his hosts by suggesting that the French people adopt a conservative rather than a radical new constitution. He warned that if France tried to leap ahead too fast, and without adequate education of the French masses, the revolution might end in a military dictatorship—which it did.

Jefferson is one of the originators of the idea of American exceptionalism, the conviction that the American experiment is fundamentally different from that of the history and destiny of other nations, that what worked for Europe will not necessarily work here, and what works here will not very likely translate to social and demographic conditions elsewhere.

Jefferson would surely argue that our duty is to study the world, master the geography, economics, and political arrangements of the planet, and appreciate the diversity of the world's social arrangements, rather than attempt to impose a monocultural pattern of political and economic development on nations with a fundamentally different history. It is hard to believe that Jefferson could support regime change, preemptive strikes, weapons of mass destruction, or the idea that dependence on foreign resources like oil could be construed to constitute an American "interest" in another sovereign nation or a region of the planet.

The course of human events over the past century (from McKinley to the Bush dynasty) has forced the United States to take seriously its place in the larger world. Without ever quite talking it through, the United States ceased to be a republic and became an empire during the twentieth century. If, in the wake of September 11, 2001, the United States is—like it or not—a central player in the troubled theater of the world, we can still be Jeffersonians if we:

⭐ bring Enlightenment idealism to our relations with the other peoples of the world;

⭐ believe in the rule of law, and the need to subordinate force to law and negotiation wherever possible, even when that course proves exceedingly frustrating;

⭐ approach the rest of the world with humility, with curiosity, with deep study, and with tolerance; understand that each nation, tribe, or culture has its own traditions, history, habits, and spirit, and that it is not for us to pretend that all peoples want to live like us. We must not presume that other peoples want to buy what we buy, watch what we watch, speak as we speak, or subordinate the life of the spirit as we do to the pursuit of material happiness;

⭐ realize that while economic activity and prosperity are important, the purpose of the world is not solely profit and power, but culture, dignity, and liberty, and the rule of law;

⭐ realize that in a world where national boundaries have been eroded by the forces of globalization, the need for distributive justice now applies to peoples throughout regions, even throughout the planet, not just to citizens of a single nation-state. In a global village characterized by intense electronic networking, until there is some equalization of the distribution of the basic fruits of life (food, shelter, basic clothing, medical care), we can expect other peoples' reaction to us to be characterized by anger, violence, illegal immigration, terrorism, and war.

A Jeffersonian takes pride in maintaining a global rather than a merely national perspective. Without ever ceasing to be a good American, a Jeffersonian feels appreciation for the customs and habits of other peoples and avoids merely carrying his or her own culture across national boundaries. Jeffersonians believe in immersion in other civilizations, and they apprehend those cultures with curiosity and wonder rather than judgment.

Jeffersonians regard foreign cultures as mirrors through which they are privileged to look at themselves with a new commitment to reason and a new understanding that at least some of our habits and systems are arbitrary, not necessarily natural or rational. Jeffersonians study foreign languages, not for the Hamiltonian purpose of increasing competitive advantage in commerce, but to attempt to see the world through the eyes of people who live by different ways and means. Jeffersonians learn Spanish to be able to read Cervantes' *Don Quixote* in the original language. They study Latin not to increase their vocabularies, but to have the pleasure of reading Horace and Vergil in their marvelous native cadences. They learn ancient Greek not to gain authority for their biblical interpretations, but to deepen their love affair with Homer and Plutarch.

Wealth and Merit

Whenever there is in any country uncultivated lands and unemployed poor, it is clear that the laws of property have been so far extended as to violate natural right. The earth is given as a common stock for man to labor and live on. If for the encouragement of industry we allow it to be appropriated, we must take care that other employment be provided to those excluded from the appropriation. If we do not, the fundamental right to labor the earth returns to the unemployed.

Jefferson to Reverend James Madison,
October 28, 1785

A **Jeffersonian** believes that the economy, left to itself, distributes the fruits of life unfairly—that a just society has no choice but to find ways to limit the excesses of capitalism, and must be prepared to redistribute wealth to a certain degree in the name of equality of circumstance. This is something of a paradox, because Jefferson did not like government, and he certainly did not believe in the set of government programs that are embraced by the terms *New Deal, welfare state,* or *Great Society.* How does a suspicious libertarian, a disciple of Adam Smith, prevent the excesses of runaway capitalism?

Jefferson hoped that American circumstances would somehow magically discourage severe inequalities in the distribution of wealth. But if unjustifiable concentrations of wealth did occur, Jefferson's reluctant solution was a graduated income tax that would serve as a disincentive to vast accumulations of wealth and would make funds available for some sort of benign redistribution downward to the less fortunate individuals of American society. Think of Sweden, perhaps, with severely graduated income taxes, but without the welfare state.

At the very least Jefferson believed that we must all agree that great differentials in wealth and material comfort are not an inevitable and therefore acceptable fact of life. Jefferson, like his friend Benjamin Franklin, regarded disproportionate accumulations of wealth as a socially derived privilege rather than a natural right of property, and he believed that we must all acknowledge, as part of our social contract, that when the gap between rich and poor gets to be too large, we have a commonwealth interest in making careful adjustments in the name of fairness.

The assumption of the conservatives of our time—that the rich deserve what they have and the poor are simply not working hard enough—would strike Jefferson as a weak-minded apology for pseudo-aristocracy and economic corruption.

Like his hero John Locke, Jefferson believed that every individual has a natural right to a farm or its economic equivalent; that humans are born with the basic right to subsistence, provided that they are willing to work to achieve it; and that any economic system that forgets this fact is a corrupt one.

Jefferson believed that while the enlightened state ought to be reluctant to interfere in the free workings of the economy, at the very least it must not lend its official energies to the protection and promotion of artificial privilege. In other words, the enlightened state errs on the side of equality rather than on the side of wealth. Jefferson believed that education is the great equalizer—that if we educate everyone to his capacity, the middle class would grow almost to the end of the spectrum on both sides (extreme wealth at one end and extreme poverty at the other), and that the problem of maldistribution of wealth would diminish, if not completely disappear. Jefferson believed that property is important but not sacrosanct.

In buying the Louisiana Territory in 1803, Jefferson believed he was acquiring a public opportunity domain of 828,000 square miles that would postpone problems of distributive justice for centuries, if not forever.

A Jeffersonian believes that a great nation champions merit rather than privilege. Jefferson called those who enjoy arbitrary success in life the "pseudo-aristocrats," and he urged the United States to legislate impediments to their ascendancy, or at the very least not prop up their privilege. As much as possible, Jefferson wanted to eliminate artificial and socially privileged distinctions between individuals and to create a level playing field on which anybody could achieve excellence if she or he showed sufficient industry. To John Adams he wrote, "May we not even say, that that form of government is the best, which provides the most effectually for a pure selection of these natural aristoi into the offices of government? The artificial aristocracy is a mischievous ingredient in government, and provision should be made to prevent its ascendancy."[7]

Jefferson knew that in any society an artificial order will emerge in which certain individuals and families will attain a prominence that has little or nothing to do with merit. Social conservatives will then come to argue that the way things are is the way things ought to be. Their view was revealingly articulated a century later by coal mine operator George Baer, an executive with the Philadelphia & Reading Railroad, who responded to labor unrest by declaring, "The rights and interests of the laboring man will be protected and cared for—not by the labor agitators, but by the Christian men to whom God in His infinite wisdom has given control of the property interests of the country." Yeah, right! Jefferson understood that the powerful and privileged will always take care of themselves, that they need no help from the state. Indeed, the danger is that they will become

---

7   Jefferson to John Adams, October 28, 1813

the state, or buy the state, or secretly replace the state. He believed that genuine merit is evenly distributed across the population base and that the state has a vital interest in nurturing merit outside the halls of privilege.

Jeffersonians never believe that they are entitled to the privileges which they nevertheless make the best use of in the interests of the commonwealth. Whether they are aristocrats by birth (those he dismissed as "pseudo-aristocrats") or privileged thanks to hard work and integrity (those he called "natural aristocrats"), they labor every day to earn again their status at the apex of American life.

Free Minds

The error seems not sufficiently eradicated, that the operations of the mind, as well as the acts of the body, are subject to the coercion of the laws. But our rulers can have no authority over such natural rights, only as we have submitted to them. The rights of conscience we never submitted, we could not submit. We are answerable for them to our God. The legitimate powers of government extend to such acts only as are injurious to others. But it does me no injury for my neighbor to say there are twenty gods, or no God. It neither picks my pocket nor breaks my leg. If it be said, his testimony in a court of justice cannot be relied on, reject it then, and be the stigma on him. Constraint may make him worse by making him a hypocrite, but it will never make him a truer man. It may fix him obstinately in his errors, but will not cure them. Reason and free inquiry are the only effectual agents against error. Give a loose to them, they will support the true religion by bringing every false one to their tribunal, to the test of their investigation. They are the natural enemies of error, and of error only.

Jefferson, *Notes on the State of Virginia*, 1785

A **Jeffersonian** believes in unlimited freedom of thought. The central principle of the Enlightenment was that no idea had special status, no idea need be protected from scrutiny. The Enlightenment argued for a free marketplace of ideas, where all ideas would be permitted to compete for the hearts and minds of the public without the slightest censorship. In the preamble to his Virginia Statute for Religious Liberty (1786), Jefferson argued that the only ideas that required government support were suspect ones. Jefferson envisioned a nation of robust discourse, with a cheerful commitment to dissent.

As the twenty-first century unfolds, Americans have a paradoxical relationship with free thought and free speech. On the one hand, we have more incidental freedom than any people who have ever lived. We can travel at will throughout the United States, and slip into the profoundest anonymity in almost any locality; publish or purchase obnoxious, irresponsible, pornographic, bigoted, racist, murderous, and seditious tracts; and shout publicly that the president or the chief justice of the Supreme Court or the bishop of the Catholic Church is a thief, warmonger, swine, imbecile, pederast, or foreign agent—all this with perfect legal impunity. We can purchase virtually anything anywhere on credit, and our associations are almost never regulated in any way. We can consume as many of the earth's resources as we can afford to pay for. We can profess any religious sensibility, from the dourest Presbyterianism to the most sensualist New Age massage cultism, from radical double predestination to Wicca eroticism— all without the slightest governmental interference, and with tax exemption to boot. By the standards of the Age of Jefferson, we are breathtakingly free, freer than any people who ever walked the earth.

On the other hand, as all foreign visitors (beginning with Alexis de Tocqueville, in 1831–32) realize, there is a numbing homogeneity to American thought. Left entirely free to think for ourselves, we have permitted our capitalist systems of dissemination to squeeze our free minds into severely limited channels. In fact, we invite it. We are free, but we freely watch the same television programs, buy the same products because of the obscene illusion—now universal in our advertising—that our soul's restlessness can be assuaged by the purchase of Brand X. We have voluntarily enslaved ourselves to the jejune, the superficial, and the faddish. Americans are free, but they are not intellectually mature or culturally sophisticated. Perhaps it is fear of the vast outback of our intellectual freedom that impels us to cluster together in a handful of cultural clearings, and to volunteer to be sheep-like even though there is no determined shepherd in our midst. The good Jeffersonian is always disappointed to find that her or his mind is gravitating to conventional wisdom and faddish notions.

The twenty-first century will present us with the greatest (perhaps final) test of the ideals of the Enlightenment. The electronic revolution has brought about a discourse infrastructure in which anyone can post any idea in public space at any time, without peer review or the cumbersomeness and expense of the publishing technologies of the past. A breathtaking chaos of ideas will take their place on the stage of twenty-first-century life, and no institution, public or private, will be able to police that stage to limit or forbid the worst excesses of free expression: sedition, corrosive cynicism, character assassination, disclosure of industrial secrets, disclosure of weapons design, theft of intellectual property (which will come to be seen as a quaint notion from the past), pornography, hate speech, unrestrained dogmatics, or exploitation of the powerless.

In a sense the new world of the electronic revolution will call the bluff of the ideals of the Enlightenment and make us ask ourselves if we really desire a "free marketplace of ideas." Given the abuses that are guaranteed to characterize this new order of the ages (*novus ordo seclorum*), the temptation will be to back away from the libertarian model of discourse and establish some form of thought policing. This the Jeffersonian must resist, however difficult that conviction makes her or his life. We are going to have to get serious about public education and the humanities if we do not wish to be that thing that Jefferson most feared, "a nation ignorant and [temporarily] free."[8]

---

8   Jefferson to Charles Yancey, January 6, 1816

A Jeffersonian believes in the Archimedean power of education and—in spite of all the evidence—continues to be the champion of the public education system in the United States. Jefferson warned us that we could not be a nation of ignorant, disengaged, low-information citizens. No honest person can deny our national ignorance as the twenty-first century unfolds. We are today the most ill-educated great nation in the world, indeed the most ill-educated great nation in human history. Jefferson believed that in a republic every individual needs to be educated up to his or her capacity. The widespread anti-intellectual streak in the American character would have seemed to Jefferson not only self-defeating, but the death knell of anything like an American republic.

Suspicious of positive government (the welfare state), Jefferson believed that education is the panacea—that almost all social ills will disappear in a better informed and better educated nation. In the face of all the perceived problems of American life, Jefferson would almost certainly argue that education is the answer to each one of them, infinitely preferable to regulation, taxation, reparation, or the appropriation of money for new applications of the welfare state.

For Jefferson, education is not merely book learning. Although he was one of the best-educated men in American history, Jefferson was a thoroughgoing pragmatist who believed that the practical arts (such as agriculture, seamanship, and craftwork) were every bit as important as political theory or Greek grammar. Jefferson was the founder of the University of Virginia, but he is also considered the father of the community and junior college system, vocational education, and (with Dr. Franklin) public libraries, including the Library of Congress. Theory and metaphysics frustrated him. He embodied the spirit of the American Philosophical Society (founded 1743), which was dedicated to the promotion of useful knowledge.

Jefferson considered his father, Peter's, desire that he be fully and classically educated to be more important than any material inheritance he might have received. He was committed to lifelong learning, and he seems to have believed not that education is a preparation for life, but that it is a *way of life* in an enlightened world, especially in a society that has committed itself to self-government. The Jeffersonian is a severe autodidact who looks upon the years of formal education merely as a foundation for the decades of hard study and reading that almost alone redeem life from its tedium and its many social and biological setbacks.

Jefferson was not in any way hostile to private education, but he would be rigidly antagonistic to the idea of spending public money to support private education. Jefferson sought to maintain a wall of separation between public and private ventures (the burden in public ventures is universal accessibility and equality), and he believed that the public school was a kind of miniature laboratory of democracy, where the children of rich and poor, Jew and Gentile, farmer and merchant, genius and plodder met under conditions of mutual respect and tolerance.

Religious Freedom

Believing with you that religion is a matter which lies solely between man and his God, that he owes account to none other for his faith or his worship, that the legislative powers of government reach actions only, and not opinions, I contemplate with sovereign reverence that act of the whole American people which declared that their legislature should "make no law respecting an establishment of religion, or prohibiting the free exercise there- of," thus building a wall of separation between Church and State. Adhering to this expression of the supreme will of the nation in behalf of the rights of conscience, I shall see with sincere satisfaction the progress of those sentiments which tend to restore to man all his natural rights, convinced he has no natural right in opposition to his social duties.

Jefferson to the Danbury Baptists, *January 1, 1802*

A **Jeffersonian** is firmly committed to the "wall of separation between church and state." However much it may annoy conservatives and evangelicals, the Jeffersonian gently but firmly insists that there is no place in the public square for crosses, prayer, nativity scenes, the ten commandments, the pledge of allegiance (offensive to a Jeffersonian on other grounds, as well), or any other paeans to the Judeo-Christian tradition or any other religious system. A Jeffersonian resists—with historical evidence—the silly but still widely-espoused notion that the Founding Fathers intended a Christian commonwealth. To be sure, most of the Founding Fathers were Christians, and many of them believed that God's providence shone in some special way on the American experiment. But most of them understood that the government of the United States needed to be punctiliously neutral on questions of conscience and religion, that a citizen's religious sensibilities were entirely private, and that any governmental endorsement of religious activity, even ecumenical religious activity, was a quasi-establishment of an official religion, and therefore impermissible in a free society.

In spite of all that some evangelicals pretend, the Constitution of the United States is entirely silent on questions of religion. God is never mentioned in the Constitution, not even as the "Creator" or "Nature's God" (both from the Declaration of Independence). A Jeffersonian believes that the federal judiciary rightly interprets the meaning of the First Amendment as prohibiting virtually all overt religious expression in the public arena, and firmly denies the notion that the judicial decisions of the second half of the twentieth century deliberately misread the Constitution to promote a secularist agenda that the Founding Fathers would have found abhorrent.

Jeffersonians believe that if the evangelicals don't like the increasing enforcement of the secularist intent of the Founding Fathers, they should create a movement to amend the Constitution or tear it up altogether. Short of that, they should go about their private (and absolutely unmolested) worship in private spaces (chapels, synagogues, mosques, churches, private schools, summer camps), and show more respect for the social compact.

Jeffersonians are freethinkers, skeptics, and rationalists, which means that if they are Christians, they tend to be nominal and habitual Christians rather than believers in the divinity of Jesus. Jefferson believed that Jesus was one of the greatest men who ever lived, certainly the greatest ethicist, and that a simple adherence to Jesus' ethical code would bring about paradise on earth, but that the metaphysics of Christianity—from the miracles to the apocalypse, from original sin to the Trinity or the efficacy of prayer—were primitive inherited mythologies or deliberate or inadvertent misreadings of the biblical texts that embarrass the validity of Jesus' message, and which can (and should) be discarded by beings worthy of the title "rational." Jefferson did not insist on deistic Unitarianism for others, but he assumed things were headed in that direction.

Even so, Jefferson respected the religious sensibilities of all un-self-righteous others, and defended to the death their right to worship any god they pleased, so long as they did not try to prescribe religious activity for others.

The Jeffersonian is a one-person ACLU, politely but firmly insisting upon the utter neutrality of the state with respect to questions of conscience.

The Pursuit of Happiness

I am savage enough to prefer the woods, the wilds, and the independence of Monticello to all the brilliant pleasures of this gay capital. I shall, therefore, rejoin myself to my native country with new attachments and with exaggerated esteem for its advantages; for though there is less wealth there, there is more freedom, more ease, and less misery.

Jefferson to Baron de Geismar, *September 6, 1785*

I had rather be shut up in a very modest cottage, with my books, my family and a few old friends, dining on simple bacon, and letting the world roll on as it liked than to occupy the most splendid post which any human power can give.

Jefferson to Alexander Donald, *February 7, 1788*

A **Jeffersonian** believes in the good life. Jefferson considered himself an Epicurean, though in the severely virtuous rather than hedonistic sense of the term. He surrounded himself with beauty: in architecture, in his gardens and fields, in his books and furnishings, in art and in music. There was, in Iago's words, "a daily beauty in his life" that ought to inspire us to live with something like equal dignity and happiness.

Monticello is a world of rich textures, excellent sight lines, beautiful vistas, symmetrical design motifs, and lovely accoutrements. It is a mountaintop sanctuary for a profusion of fruits, vegetables, grains, flowers, vineyards, and orchards. Jefferson was incapable of living with the mediocre, the imprecise, or the mundane. He brought an exquisite sensibility to all that he ever did. In a sense it is a pity that he lived part of his life in the political arena, because there least of all could he shape the contours of his world into sweet harmony. He longed for the harmonies of Monticello, far away from and above the rancorous jostlings in the political arena. He lamented that politics is a crude, aggressive, and messy business, and he infinitely preferred to live his life in a world of decanters, books, cabinets, scientific instruments, and family.

Jefferson believed that we exist to be happy, not to struggle through life or perform duties or deny ourselves pleasures. There is nothing dour or Calvinist in the Jeffersonian temperament. No day should unfold without the pleasures of food, wine, nature, flowers, exercise, correspondence, family, friendship, books, art, music, and contemplation. And love. His motto was "Take things always by their smooth handle." Jefferson was a thoroughgoing rationalist who believed that one of the keys to happiness was the avoidance of conflict and pain. "Do not bite at the bait of pleasure till you know there is no hook beneath it," he wrote in his famous love letter to Maria Cosway, "My Head and My Heart" (October 12, 1786). "The art of life is the art of avoiding pain: and he is the best pilot who steers clearest of the rocks and shoals with which it is beset. The most effectual means of being secure against pain is to retire within ourselves, and to suffice for our own happiness." This was the stoic strain in Jefferson's character, born of a classical education and an early and profound experience of pain and loss.

The Jeffersonian has a highly evolved aesthetic sense. To enter his or her world is to understand that the accoutrements of life are a measure of the quality of one's soul, and that it is the duty of mature human beings to surround themselves with objects and structures that declare to the world what is really valuable—and lovely. One need only examine a single Jefferson document—choose one at random—to see the exquisiteness of his penmanship and the delicacy of his temperament. Or spend an hour in his Cabinet of Curiosities, his "Indian Hall" at Monticello, to see what he valued, collected, and interpreted. His letters are works of art in both senses: they show an immense epistolary artistry, and they are beautiful to look at irrespective of the meaning of the words they present to the world.

Jeffersonians prefer the art of living to power, success, wealth, or status. And they pursue friendship.

A Jeffersonian is an excellent friend. Thomas Jefferson had a gigantic capacity for friendship. He saw the world through the twin lenses of large Enlightenment abstractions ("all men are created equal") and harmonious friendship. He had a gift for placing himself in the mindset of his friends, understanding their sensibilities, sympathizing with the complexities of their lives, and anticipating their wants. He wrote to his friends often, generously, and with a deep respect for their souls. He was intensely loyal. In many respects, he understood that friendship is the highest form of human relationship—voluntary, based on affinity and shared values, and uncluttered by the dense emotions and dysfunctions of family life. Jefferson's closest adult friend was James Madison, but a list of his friends would occupy many pages of text. Among them were James Monroe, John Adams, Abigail Adams, Thomas Paine, Maria Cosway, Benjamin Franklin, Meriwether Lewis, Charles Willson Peale, George Washington, John Page, Dabney Carr, Elizabeth Trist, John Taylor, Benjamin Rush, David Rittenhouse, Joseph Priestley, Lafayette, and Benjamin Smith Barton. Somehow Jefferson had the talent of making each of his friends feel especially important, loved, and central to his happiness. Jefferson's daughter Martha said her father never gave up a friend—or an opinion.

Jeffersonians love friendship and pay special attention to its many satisfactions. They try to give their best energies to their friends, and they spend time devising ways to find perfect gifts for them, serve their interests, listen to their concerns, and resonate fully with their souls. They measure the world according to the friendships they form, and they seek friendship not for what it can do for their careers or their public lives, but for what it can do for their private pursuit of happiness.

Science and Knowledge

I am for encouraging the progress of science in all it's branches; and not for raising a hue and cry against the sacred name of philosophy, [not] for awing the human mind by stories of raw-head & bloody bones to a distrust of its own vision, & to repose implicitly on that of others; [not] to go backwards instead of forwards to look for improvement; to believe that government, religion, morality, & every other science were in the highest perfection in ages of the darkest ignorance, and that nothing can ever be devised more perfect than what was established by our forefathers.

Jefferson to Elbridge Gerry, January 26, 1799

A **Jeffersonian** believes in the primacy of science. Although Jefferson (reluctantly and somewhat inadvertently) helped to create our political party system, he found partisanship repulsive and believed that most human problems lend themselves to common-sense, nonpartisan solutions. He believed that science (knowledge) is virtually infallible, that the more knowledge we accumulate, the more intelligent will be our solutions to problems. He would be appalled by the politicization of science in our time—with the result that each side in a lawsuit lines up "experts" not to speak the truth as they perceive it but to promote a certain point of view, and that on such questions as global climate change, the effect of acid rain, evolution, and the usefulness of stem cell research, "scientists" are inevitably lined up on both sides to say mutually-exclusive things—for hire.

Jefferson understood, of course, that not all scientists will agree on all subjects, but he believed their core commitment to objectivity and truth would produce substantial consensus on most issues. Jefferson would be disposed to defer to the dictates of science on virtually every issue.

The gigantic advances of science between 1826 and 2020 would have thrilled Jefferson. Except for quantum indeterminacy, the progress of science has vindicated Jefferson's view that there is almost nothing that is not knowable. Today he would be disposed to believe even more completely that man is essentially (as Baron d'Holbach argued) a very ingenious kind of machine, the workings of which we will come to understand with greater and greater clarity in the course of time, with the result that illness (including the kind of mental instability that bedeviled his son-in-law Thomas Mann Randolph and his protégé Meriwether Lewis) would be made to disappear altogether. Jefferson was a profound materialist who believed that the soul is corpuscular, and that there is no independent "soul" or spirit beyond the material workings of the body. This is more than many of the best scientists believe today, but Jefferson's conviction that most of the so-called mysteries of life, including moods and the workings of the brain, are capable of being understood scientifically has largely been vindicated, and it is quite likely that we are still in the incunabula of research on neuroscience and the chemistry of life.

Jefferson would be thrilled by today's space program, oceanic research, modern cartographical methods, the mapping of the genetic code, modern medicine, artificial intelligence, robotics, biochemistry, nanotechnology, crop hybridization and genetic manipulation, the possibilities of cloning, the engineering (and materials) of bridges, buildings, tunnels, and highways, irrigation systems, tracking systems, and much more. Not to mention computers.

And he would know that in essential respects we are still living in the adolescence of the engineering revolution. The twenty-first century is already breathtaking, and the acceleration has only just begun.

A Jeffersonian is not afraid of science and technology. Jeffersonians are steadfastly aware of the limitations of science, and they do whatever it takes to stay close to nature in a world increasingly fabricated by inert materials, but they realize that the careful use of science and technology is infinitely preferable to any form of nostalgia or Ludditism.

Like his hero Francis Bacon, Jefferson took all knowledge (except geology) to be his province. Jefferson was a gifted amateur who could survey a field, determine latitude and longitude, draw a map, tie an artery, write learnedly on the development of English prosody, conjugate a Greek verb, conduct a systematic archaeological dig, press and classify plants, dance the minuet, write a poem, play the violin, and classify a library. That's the short list.

Jefferson is the patron saint of generalists, of gifted dilettantes, of deep dabblers, of those who eschew a narrowly focused expertise in work or in the art of living. Jefferson believed that life is nearly equally interesting on all fronts. Concentration and specialization were anathema to Thomas Jefferson. Jeffersonians are willing to try new things, and they are constantly reinventing themselves, without losing sight of their core values and ideals. A Jeffersonian reads all the book reviews as a kind of menu of which volumes to purchase or borrow in the next months, and tries to stay abreast with what is happening in the world on a range of intellectual, political, economic, practical, and social fronts. A Jeffersonian finds her or his ignorance intolerable and strives always to learn as much as can be learned given the pace and the constraints of industrial life in the twenty-first century.

Like all Renaissance women and men, a Jeffersonian is as interested in action as in ideas. There is nothing aloof or merely bookish about a Jeffersonian. Jefferson was constantly tinkering, putting his hands in the soil, working with tools, manipulating the materials of his universe to see what benefits (and joy) he might draw from them. A Jeffersonian camps one weekend and attends a conference the next, writes letters by day and dances at night, hikes, walks, runs, explores, swims, cooks, designs, decorates, travels, sews, weaves, draws, paints, builds, grows, trims, trains, communicates, and, of course, reads incessantly.

Like Jefferson, the Jeffersonian grows in energy and inspiration from all of this dizzying activity—and, like Jefferson, constantly invents new ways to increase the range and diversity of the good life.

At a time when most individuals are winding down and beginning to wait for death, Jefferson invented the University of Virginia, the darling project of his last decade. Though harmony and repose were among his most cherished values, Jefferson could not resist the urge to do one more great thing for Virginia and America with his life's energy, to create a temple in which the Enlightenment and the ideals of the American republic could find continued, indeed permanent, expression.

The Jeffersonian, like the late I. F. Stone, takes up ancient Greek late in life for the sheer pleasure of reading the dialogues of Plato. (Jefferson found no pleasure in Plato, "the foggiest brain of antiquity," but he loved Homer and Thucydides.) Jeffersonians maintain the fires of creativity and curiosity right up to the last days of their lives.

A Jeffersonian believes that the world can be made better, that every device, habit, institution, and system is capable of being redesigned to perform its function more efficiently or more delightfully, and that we must never accept inefficiency, unfairness, or corruption merely because things have always been done that way. Jefferson believed that the past is mostly a collection of mistakes, and that the traditions of a culture do not deserve any respect beyond their measurable merit. Jefferson believed that we should be prepared to sweep away imperfect systems and try something more rational or more just, and that hoary tradition is no justification to continue any habit of culture. Jefferson further believed that we should shake things up from time to time, merely to remind ourselves that nothing is inherently entitled to permanence. He was aware that such a philosophy will sometimes create chaos—but it did not seem to bother him much.

In the Declaration of Independence, Jefferson agreed that systems should not be overthrown "for light and transient causes," but his general outlook was that rational beings could and should tinker boldly with the world about them, that there is nothing sacrosanct except natural right, and that as long as reformers remember that their duty is to improve the world for the benefit of all mankind, they should not be unduly constrained by the dead hand of the past.

When Jefferson saw an inefficient plow in the course of his European travels, he sat down immediately to design an improved plowshare, the "moldboard of least resistance." He was not afraid to reform America's coinage, her land survey and tenure systems, the existing metric system, Senate parliamentary procedures, the workings of John Hawkins' polygraph, the university curriculum, or existing library classification systems. He even adjusted the strictures of his beloved Andrea Palladio in designing Monticello and Poplar Forest.

A Jeffersonian believes that most of the "softwares" of the world are artificial constructions, not infallible echoes of the natural structure of life, and that they should be cheerfully discarded the moment a more rational, more efficient, more just, or more practical system can be devised or discerned. Jeffersonians are rational busybodies who are always asking, "Can it be improved, for whose benefit, and at what cost?"

Nature

There is not a sprig of grass that shoots uninteresting to me.
Jefferson to Martha Jefferson Randolph,
December 23, 1790

Walking is the best possible exercise. Habituate yourself to walk very far. The Europeans value themselves on having subdued the horse to the uses of man; but I doubt whether we have not lost more than we have gained by the use of this animal.
Jefferson to Peter Carr, August 19, 1785

A **Jeffersonian** is a lover of nature. Jefferson walked almost every day. Or rode a horse. Or worked in his fields or his gardens. In Jefferson's day more than 90 percent of all Americans lived on farms. Most Americans were, therefore, infinitely closer to nature than we are in the twenty-first century. Jefferson believed that life close to nature makes humans saner, wiser, happier, and more virtuous than life at any remove from the earth. That's why he called farmers "the chosen people of God." But he also purchased the Natural Bridge in western Virginia (1774) because he wanted to protect from adverse development what he considered one of the most sublime places in America. In a sense Jefferson was the father of the National Park System, because he believed that America exhibited nature in her finest and least disturbed form and that it is in our national interest to preserve the sublime for the refreshment of the human spirit.

Jefferson believed that nature redeems, restores, and reclaims humanity, and that nature is where we observe natural law in its most organic form. In other words, nature is not for Jefferson just a Wordsworthian playground for meditation and renewal, but also the best possible teacher of what is good and valuable in the world. Nature, in short, is the fundamental legislator. We put our hands in the soil to make contact with the surest guide to life, and the supreme teacher of humility and good sense. We go to nature to discern the Newtonian laws of everything.

Most Jeffersonians would like to live on farms, but don't. They do tend to grow a few things, however, no matter how confined or urban their living space. It is not the quantity that counts, but the commitment to let nature's fecundity and nature's cycles influence the rhythms of our lives that makes us Jeffersonians. Today, Jeffersonians are as apt to listen to nature in their walks, on sojourns in the national parks, national forests, national wildlife refuges, and wilderness, while camping, hiking, riding horses, kayaking rivers, and mountain climbing, as in growing food. The important thing is that Jeffersonians can never stay away from nature in one of its primary forms for very long.

Jeffersonians agree with the master's commitment to stewardship. Jefferson introduced a seven-year crop rotation system to his farms to protect them from the havoc of corn and tobacco monoculture. Along with his son-in-law Thomas Mann Randolph, he introduced contour plowing in Albemarle County. He planted shelter belts. He criticized his fellow Virginians for preferring to open new fields rather than to bring true husbandry to what they already had. "The earth belongs in usufruct to the living,"[9] Jefferson declared to James Madison, by which he meant that we have a natural right to the fruits of the earth, but we do not have the right to impair the fruitfulness of the earth. In other words, Jeffersonians are inevitably not just lovers

---

9   Jefferson to James Madison, September 6, 1789

of nature, but conservationists. Jeffersonians necessarily practice a moderate variety of environmentalism, because they agree with the Sage of Monticello that natural resources exist to serve the needs of humankind, now and forever, and that government is not the best judge of which resources shall be exploited and which left alone.

The important thing is that nature matters to Jeffersonians and they get themselves out into the open air as often and as purely as possible. They are friends to nature, they argue from nature, and they do what they can to make sure that nature continues to be available for the benefit of all Americans.

A Jeffersonian is indefatigably active and a lover of the outdoors. Jefferson's idea of relaxation was a long walk in nature or a horseback ride, or a swath of time spent puttering in the garden in the cool of the evening. He believed that idleness is the parent of ennui, melancholia, depression, error, self-indulgence, and what his Christian friends called sin. To his daughter Martha, he wrote, "Determine never to be idle. No person will have occasion to complain of the want of time who never loses any. It is wonderful how much may be done if we are always doing."[10] The idea of "kicking back," vacationing on the beach at Cabo, spending an evening eating and drinking in a tavern, or attending a football game (much less a tailgate party) would hold no appeal for Jefferson, who believed that the world is so utterly fascinating that only a fool would succumb to idleness when she or he could be reading, writing, growing something, or designing something instead. Jefferson believed that unrelenting activity was a source of energy for still more unrelenting activity.

Jefferson was something of an efficiency expert, and he took pleasure in constructing grids of how his own time might be made better use of. He never ducked an opportunity to lay out a course of reading—and of life discipline—for his friends and protégés. How

---

10   To Martha (Patsy) Jefferson, May 5, 1787

he would have thrilled to the organizational tools of our time: smart phones, GPS units, Excel charts, Apple watches and Fitbits, eBooks, digital scanning, and Skype. One need merely imagine Jefferson with a scanner and a laptop computer connected to the internet to feel his ecstasy. He made the most of the low-tech tools of his own time. Imagine what he would have done with ours. Imagine how much he would fret over our inefficient and narcissistic use of these magnificent tools—cat memes, outtakes, and porn. Americans frequently ask how much a man of such enormous accomplishment could have slept. The answer is that Jefferson slept more than most geniuses because he believed in the importance of good sense and moderation. There is nothing of the tortured artist in Jefferson's character. Jefferson's view was that it doesn't really matter how many hours one sleeps at night. What matters is what one does with her or his waking hours.

A Jeffersonian believes in the dignity and primacy of family agriculture. Long live North Dakota! In Jefferson's time, more than nine out of ten American people lived on self-sufficiency farms. Because they fed themselves, clothed themselves, and sheltered themselves, these farmers exemplified the self-reliance that Jefferson believed is the essential quality of a good citizen in a republic.

Jefferson believed that nature is the great teacher of humankind, that life at its core is actually quite simple, that the macrobiotic business of life is more important than politics or opera or even great literature. So he had a very special place in his heart and his philosophy for family farmers. Jefferson's wisest words were, "Those who labor in the earth are the chosen people of God, if ever He had a chosen people, whose breasts He has made His peculiar deposit for substantial and genuine virtue."[11]

Today only 2 percent of the American people live on family farms, and most of them are Hamiltonian agri-producers rather

---

11   Notes on Virginia, see below

than the sort of subsistence-plus farmers that Jefferson had in mind. The first fully automated farms are in the works, thus ensuring that we remove *culture* from agriculture. Most Jeffersonians do not live on farms nowadays, but they honor family farmers as a kind of irreplaceable rump of especially important citizens who can remind us of things that the rest of us tend to forget or ignore. They also see family farmers as the historically most important exemplars of the dignity of honest labor and of the nation that Jefferson intended and would still probably advocate in spite of the social, technological, and economic revolutions that have occurred since his time.

A Life in Letters

To read the Latin and Greek authors in their original is a sublime luxury; and I deem luxury in science to be at least as justifiable as in architecture, painting, gardening, or the other arts. I enjoy Homer in his own language infinitely beyond Pope's translation of him. . . . I thank on my knees him who directed my early education for having put into my possession this rich source of delight; and I would not exchange it for anything which I could then have acquired, and have not since acquired.
Jefferson to Joseph Priestley, *January 27, 1800*

A **Jeffersonian** is a writer of letters. Jefferson's basic form of communication, and his basic method of making sense of life, was the friendly letter. He wrote at least 22,000 of them with quill (eventually steel-nibbed) pens and expensive paper. Indeed, it may fairly be said that Jefferson was happiest when he was alone in a room with the English language, a book, and a blank sheet of paper before him. In our late or post-literate age, it is tempting to prize other, more immediate, forms of communication. But the fact remains that there is nothing to compare with sending or receiving a physical letter, in an envelope, with a stamp affixed, delivered by a human postal worker.

Jefferson knew that staying in touch is an essential ingredient of power. His letters were designed to keep the lines of communication—and trust, friendship, respect, and obligation—open. He knew that the greatest engine of misunderstanding and disputatiousness is a lapse into silence. He kept up his end, and he constantly rebuked his correspondents, particularly family members, for failing to write him as often, as fully, and as minutely as he desired.

Jeffersonians are intelligent enough not to turn their backs on cell phones, texts, Dropbox, and email, of course. But they know that there is no greater gesture of true regard, or satisfaction for that matter, than the sending and receiving of handwritten letters.

A Jeffersonian believes that books are at the center of any full and mature life. Thomas Jefferson approached life essentially through books. He obtained between seven and ten thousand of them in the course of his lifetime, at a time when books were rare and extremely expensive. Reading was one of his favorite activities. He prepared himself for adult life with the severest possible course of reading. For a significant period of his life, from about the age of fifteen to twenty-five, Jefferson essentially read every waking minute of every day. With the possible exceptions of Theodore Roosevelt and John Quincy Adams, Jefferson was intellectually the best-prepared president in American history.

Jefferson believed in the good sense of the American people, that no matter what their educational attainments, the mass of people would always exhibit enough good sense to govern themselves intelligently. But he knew, too, that the great texts of Western civilization provide indispensable clues about the ways to achieve and preserve human liberty, not to mention happiness. History not only teaches us what bad government has been, but also how to use the sad record of the past to envision and fight for a more enlightened future. To John Brazier Jefferson wrote, "It is often said there have been shining examples of men of great abilities, in all businesses of life, without any other science [i.e., knowledge] than what they had gathered from conversation and intercourse with the world. But, who can say what these men would not have been, had they started in the science on the shoulders of a Demosthenes or Cicero, of a Locke, or Bacon, or a Newton?"

Jefferson's reading habits were eclectic, but he clearly preferred nonfiction, and his immense library was essentially a reference collection. What Jefferson wanted most was information, facts, data points, and statistics. He saw books primarily as information delivery systems. He would be pleased at the size, scope, and accessibility of the public library system in the United States and thrilled at the internet. The English Wikipedia alone now delivers six million articles, free, to anyone on earth at any time. The fifteenth print edition of the great Encyclopedia Britannica (2007) had fewer than 100,000 articles.

Even so, Jefferson loved books as books, and regarded them as sensuous objects, and even works of art. He made sure that his beloved books were elegantly and sumptuously bound, shelved in aesthetic good taste, and classified intelligently. Unlike his disputatious friend John Adams, Jefferson did not deface his books with hectic scribbling. His marginalia were mostly confined to careful correction of spelling and grammar in the volumes he accumulated. He loved fine (expensive) paper, good ink, and handsome typography. On average, books were in Jefferson's time dramatically more pleasant to hold and caress and pore over than the books of our time. When Jefferson said he could not live without books, he meant it. It is just so with Jeffersonians.

Pragmatism

The plan of reading which I have formed [for my daughter Martha] is considerably different from that which I think would be most proper for her sex in any other country than America. I am obliged to extend my views beyond herself, and consider her as the head of a little family of her own. The chance that in marriage she will draw a blockhead I calculate at about fourteen to one, and of course that the education of her family will probably rest on her own ideas and directions without assistance.
Jefferson to François de Barbé-Marbois, *December 5, 1783*

A **Jeffersonian** is a pragmatic idealist, and a practical utopian. Jefferson's enemies called him "philosopher," "dreamer," and "utopian." He was regarded as a Platonic philosopher, "fast asleep in philosophical tranquility," while more practical men like Madison and John Adams did what they could to anchor him to the real world. And yet Jefferson reformed our coinage, built a university out of brick and marble, created a rectilinear survey grid system that organized our entire Western national development, and tinkered incessantly with gadgets and labor-saving devices. He had the capacity to state the universal truth on such questions as freedom of the press or the right to revolution, but he had a deep distaste for metaphysics or mere abstraction. He dreamed of an American pastoral utopia, but he worked hard to raise funds for a canal that would link the Potomac River to the American interior. He was a fascinating mix of the universal and the concrete. It is never possible to dismiss him as a "utopian," for few dreamers ever accomplished as much in the real world.

Jeffersonians know that half a loaf is better than none. They dream of an America in which everyone is educated to her or his capacity, where citizens are eternally vigilant, where science rules, and where people pursue happiness and dignity and the life of the mind rather than storm a new shopping mall on the day of its grand opening. But they also fight to keep *Catcher in the Rye* or *Slaughterhouse Five* from being banned by the local school district, and they help to organize day care centers in the workplace. To be a Jeffersonian is to remain an idealist in adult life without being silly or uninformed. Jeffersonians envision a second American Enlightenment, but they also work assiduously to bring about small improvements in the world around them.

In a sense, Jeffersonians work a variation on the great motto "Think Globally, Act Locally." Jeffersonians dream idealistically, but they act pragmatically. For Jefferson, and for Jeffersonians, this has proved to be an enormously attractive (and powerful) combination of energies. It is virtually the only formula for changing the world gracefully.

A Jeffersonian is a willful optimist. At a low moment, Jefferson wrote, "I am born to lose everything I love."[12] Four of his six white children died in their infancy. A fifth, his younger daughter Maria (Polly), died in 1804 at the age of twenty-five. Jefferson's father, mother, favorite sister Jane, and closest friend Dabney Carr all died prematurely by twenty-first century standards.

Jefferson lived in serious debt through most of his adult life, and by 1815 the debt was so massive that he was barely able to maintain enough solvency to live out his life at Monticello. This was a source— occasionally—of great stress in Jefferson's life. At any given moment

---

12   To Martha Jefferson Randolph, July 17, 1790

after his second term as president, Jefferson was in a position to realize that his lifestyle was economically insupportable, and that if he actually lived within his means, he would be forced to sell off almost everything he owned, including perhaps Monticello, and that he would need to forego many of his most cherished habits of accumulation and consumption: fine imported wines, books, music and musical instruments, furnishings and finishing hardware for his building projects, housewares, works of art, and much more.

Jefferson knew that his ownership of slaves, his need to buy and sell slaves, hunt them down when they ran away, have them whipped for insubordination, and evade pointed questions put to him by his Enlightenment friends about his dependency on an institution they all agreed was morally and legally repugnant, was a blot upon his reputation as an advocate for human rights. He must have known that the judgment of history was bound to catch up with him, and condemn him for violating the very codes for which he was the foremost articulator of his time, and perhaps of all time.

Jefferson spoke frequently of the joys and harmony of his family life, but behind the agreeable rhetoric lay a highly dysfunctional family.

Jefferson's daughter Martha's husband, Thomas Mann Randolph, had a flash temper, and he was subject to nervous fits and periods of alienation from home, family, and community. Jefferson's sons-in-law (particularly the mercurial Randolph) were engaged in a struggle for the affection and respect of their father-in-law, and both daughters strained to keep their father central to their lives and hearts (as he wished it) without making it impossible for them to bond fully with their husbands.

The specter of debt and decay hung over Monticello from 1809 onward. Jefferson's granddaughter Ann married an abusive man who beat her and, as a consequence, became involved in a public brawl with Jefferson's grandson Thomas Jefferson Randolph in downtown Charlottesville. Jefferson's daughter Martha's sister-in-law was involved in a notorious adulterous liaison which ended in alleged infanticide and a spectacular public trial that embarrassed everyone it touched. It was not, in short, all Palladian neoclassicism in Albemarle County, Virginia, whatever Jefferson might say in his voluminous correspondence. Jefferson's Virginia world was in many respects closer to *Gone with the Wind* than Horatian Arcadia.

And yet, Jefferson somehow remained optimistic right up to the end.

Some of Jefferson's optimism was temperamental, but more was the result of a deliberate choice. His private Decalogue (1825) indicates how important will was in his pursuit of happiness. Here are a few of his commandments.

🌟 Never put off till to-morrow what you can do to-day.

🌟 Never trouble another for what you can do yourself.

🌟 Nothing is troublesome that we do willingly.

🌟 How much pain have cost us the evils which have never happened.

🌟 Take things always by their smooth handle.[13]

Like Franklin and Washington, Jefferson set out early in life to discipline his soul and rub off the rough edges from his character. He believed in self-mastery. He believed that a person of self-restraint could avoid the spasms of irrational behavior that bring chaos and suffering to life. Avoidance of crisis brings peace and harmony to one's existence, and a sustained period of harmony leads one to be optimistic about the prospects of life. In other words, some part of Jeffersonian optimism was the result of leading a life of rational calculation, rather than impulse. It also involved a commitment to social harmony.

In a letter to his favorite grandson, Thomas Jefferson Randolph, Jefferson recommended that the boy adopt "artificial good humor."

In truth, politeness is artificial good humor, it covers the natural want of it, and ends by rendering habitual a substitute nearly

---

13   To Thomas Jefferson Smith, February 21, 1825

equivalent to the real virtue. It is the practice of sacrificing to those whom we meet in society, all the little conveniences and preferences which will gratify them, and deprive us of nothing worth a moment's consideration; it is the giving a pleasing and flattering turn to our expressions, which will conciliate others, and make them pleased with us as well as themselves. How cheap a price for the good will of another![14]

Jefferson appears to have passed through eighty-three years without often (perhaps ever) lapsing into rudeness and aggression. He was essentially a character out of a Jane Austen novel: civil, graceful, polite, well-mannered, reasonable, euphemistic, and poised. He subscribed to some variation of the golden rule: He who treats others with civility and generosity will usually be treated well in return, and the result of this tacit quid pro quo is that there are fewer blows to one's cheerful view of life.

Perhaps Jefferson adopted artificial good humor or optimism as a way to counterbalance all the losses and setbacks of his life. One senses that below the serene Palladian surface of Jefferson's persona was a more volatile, at times volcanic, emotional life, and that Jefferson set out—at some early point in his life—to achieve stoic imperturbability in order to avoid letting his emotions run away with his peace of mind. Late in life Jefferson lamented to John Adams that he had known almost unbearable losses. "There are, I acknolege, even in the happiest life, some terrible convulsions, heavy set-offs against the opposite page of the account," he admitted, but almost immediately he returned to his willful optimism. "I think with you that it is a good world, on the whole; that it has been framed on a principle of benevolence, and more pleasure than pain dealt out to us. There are, indeed (who might say nay), gloomy and hypochondriac minds, inhabitants of diseased bodies, disgusted with the present

---

14   To Thomas Jefferson Randolph, November 24, 1808

and despairing of the future, always counting that the worst will happen because it may happen."[15]

Whatever the cause, it is indisputable that Jefferson spent virtually no time indulging in negativity.

It was entirely rational that an Enlightenment philosopher like Jefferson looked upon the future with optimism. As he put it in his first inaugural address, the United States possessed "a chosen country, with room enough for our descendants to the thousandth and thousandth generation." He believed that the Atlantic Ocean was a 3,000-mile moat that separated the pastoral innocence of America from the madness, havoc, and the dark history of the Old World. He was nearly in solidarity with Thomas Paine when the great pamphleteer proclaimed that "we have it in our power to begin the world over again."

Surely Jefferson believed that he was living in the best of all possible times, in what would soon become the best of all republics in the best of all possible worlds—worlds providentially designed by a benign Newtonian god. The North American continent, meanwhile, was from a white European point of view both a tabula rasa upon which the Americans were destined to write their utopia, and the most stupendous treasury of untapped resources on earth. No nation, Jefferson believed, had ever begun its rendezvous with destiny with so many incontestable advantages. In Jefferson's mind, any American who could see all this and remain a pessimist was fit only for an asylum. When former president George H. W. Bush used to respond to doubt by effusing, "We're America!" he was articulating the Jeffersonian optimism. And mine.

The only note of shadow in this American Arcadia came, appropriately, from the deepening crisis over slavery. To John Holmes, Jefferson wrote on April 22, 1820, "I regret that I am now to die in the belief, that the useless sacrifice of themselves by the

---

15   To John Adams, April 8, 1816

generation of 1776, to acquire self-government and happiness to their country, is to be thrown away by the unwise and unworthy passions of their sons, and that my only consolation is to be, that I live not to weep over it."[16] Whether Jefferson's bitterness reflected his own moral paralysis in the face of his complicity in slavery is unknowable, but all students of Jefferson search for the moral fallout from this, the greatest of his inconsistencies.

In the face of the madness and the destructiveness of the twentieth century, Jefferson's belief in the essential "goodness of man" can seem fatuous, perhaps even infantile. Between Freud and Hitler and Pol Pot and Hiroshima, the Enlightenment's rosy picture of human nature and the human project was dealt fundamental and perhaps fatal blows. If Jefferson could believe that all rational beings perceive the benevolence of things, a similarly confident social observer today might argue that all rational beings must be disenchanted realists—believers that humankind is born to botch the world.

The appropriate Jeffersonian response at the beginning of the twenty-first century would seem to be an Augustinian diagnosis and a sober but hopeful Jeffersonianism prescription. In other words, today's Jeffersonians ought to acknowledge that human nature—if human behavior is a fair measure—is often an open indictment of the Enlightenment's optimism, and yet there is good reason to believe that under the right circumstances the world can be made better to a considerable degree. Jefferson subscribed to the indefinite—not the complete—perfectibility of humankind.

---

16   Jefferson to John Holmes, April 22, 1820

Leadership

The ground of liberty is to be gained by inches, that we must be contented to secure what we can get from time to time, and eternally press forward for what is yet to get. It takes time to persuade men to do even what is for their own good.

Jefferson to Charles Clay, *January 27, 1790*

My great wish is to go on in a strict but silent performance of my duty: to avoid attracting notice & to keep my name out of newspapers, because I find the pain of a little censure, even when it is unfounded, is more acute than the pleasure of much praise.

Jefferson to Francis Hopkinson, *March 12, 1789*

A Jeffersonian is a natural, albeit reluctant, leader. Although he preferred to be home at Monticello among his gardens, grandchildren, orchards, and books, Jefferson held nearly every office available in the United States in his time. Reluctant though he was, he was the master leader of his generation, and he managed somehow to stay afloat through forty years of one of the most tempestuous times in American political history. Meanwhile, the two Adamses were confined to single terms, Washington had lost a good deal of national support by the time he retired, and Madison and Monroe would probably not have become president were it not for the prior leadership of Jefferson. Hamilton was unelectable and Patrick Henry remained a provincial Virginia statesman, a man better at bringing down a corrupt system than at inventing a better one. Jefferson alone bestrode the early national period like a colossus.

Jefferson was a mild-mannered leader who steadfastly refused to call attention to himself. He preferred to work by indirection. He shrank from conflicts, or at least had lieutenants handle them on his behalf, so that he could maintain his characteristic repose. Jefferson's leadership style consisted of:

⭐ great clarity of expression;

⭐ mastery of detail—he was always the best prepared person in the room;

⭐ optimism;

⭐ personal generosity and sympathy;

⭐ advocacy of the people's rights, dignity, and capacity for self-government;

⭐ steady and respectful communication with everyone he wanted to persuade.

Jefferson was not just a leader in the political arena. He was a leader in architecture, in agriculture, in science, and in literature. He seems really to have believed that the leader's duty is to "ameliorate the condition of mankind," with as little fanfare as possible, and calling as little attention to himself as possible.

Leadership is a paradoxical entity in a republic. If we believe that the people are capable of governing themselves with a minimum of top-down coordination, then little room is left for leadership in any traditional sense. Republican leaders are (seemingly?) egoless men like Jefferson, rather than heroes on horseback like Theodore Roosevelt. Jefferson prided himself on always adhering to two principles: that the rational, enlightened path is always preferable to one based on traditional assertions of power; and that it is rarely, if ever, a good idea to thwart the decided will of the people.

Jeffersonians provide leadership because they know that if the exemplars of reason and good sense abdicate their public responsibilities, the advocates of greed, force, and social hierarchy will run away with the country. Jeffersonians lead because they know that the world becomes more enlightened only if every enlightened person gives service to the commonwealth energies of the community. Jeffersonians lead because they know that social apathy is not an option if you wish to live in a republic.

Like the Sage of Monticello, Jeffersonians lead by suavity, the arts of rational persuasion, indirection, and a commitment to social harmony. They master whatever they undertake. They perennially keep in mind the desired outcome, not the primacy of their own egos. They are modest about their accomplishments, and they are reluctant to stand at the front of any group whatsoever.

A Jeffersonian leader is a mentor. Jefferson benefited from gifted mentors, and he became a collector of protégés himself. Jefferson's father, Peter, died when he was just fourteen years old. That left a hole in Jefferson's life that was never completely filled. Jefferson was fortunate that as a young man he won the affection and respect of two great mentors: William Small, professor of mathematics at the College of William and Mary; and George Wythe, the self-taught Greek and legal scholar, who practiced law in Williamsburg. Later Jefferson said Small "set the destinies of my life,"[17] by putting good books in front of him and urging him to be a genuine freethinker. Jefferson could never praise Wythe sufficiently for his commitment to classical learning and a deep rooting in the humanities.

Jefferson served as mentor to a significant number of individuals, most notably James Monroe, Meriwether Lewis, William Small, his nephew Peter Carr, and his grandson Thomas Jefferson Randolph. Jefferson saw his role as providing reading lists for gifted young men, pressing them to master languages and to read deeply and widely, and providing some carefully modulated guidance about moral development. Jefferson can be said to have politically mentored James

---

17   Jefferson, *Autobiography*, 1821

Madison (who hardly needed a mentor) and James Monroe, both of whom served in the presidency after Jefferson retired. By mentoring these two remarkable individuals, Jefferson in a sense obtained for himself a third, fourth, fifth, and sixth term as president. Madison and Monroe served their mentor in part by continuing to carry out his principles when they followed him into the presidency. The Virginia Dynasty presided over the new republic from 1801 to 1825.

Though Jefferson would not have put it quite this way, mentors have an advantage over one's parents because they are more disinterested, more emotionally detached, more purely generous.

Jeffersonians take the time to become mentors because they understand that adolescence is a perilous time in which promising young people need the help of gifted older people who wish to see them blossom into genius. They know that in many respects the world is repaired one person at a time, and that by shaping the development of one remarkable person, a mentor may in the end be shaping the development of an institution, a community, perhaps even a culture. Jeffersonians become mentors because they remember their own development, and feel deep appreciation for those who intervened at precisely the right moment to take them to a higher level of achievement and understanding.

Almost every extraordinary achiever can point to a mentor who made all the difference. That was certainly true of Jefferson and his primary mentor William Small. Although mentoring has fallen somewhat into disfavor in our time (thanks to our hypersensitivity about intimacy between older and younger people), Jeffersonians carefully persevere, knowing that the mentor-apprentice relationship is not only one of the most important, but also one of the most precious and satisfying relationships we can have.

Jefferson in 2020

It's natural and inevitable that people of our time want to know what the Founding Fathers would think about the specific issues that bedevil America today. I try not to get overly specific—how do I know what Jefferson would think about the state of Israel, or television sitcoms? Nevertheless, it is possible to have a fair amount of certainty about what his views would be. You can trust that Jefferson would decry the role of big money and political action groups in our politics. You know Jefferson would be appalled by pornography, weapons of mass destruction, and torture. But what would he think of Bitcoins? Hard to know.

Keeping my sense of caution in mind, I will attempt to respond to a few specific questions that are routinely put to me regarding how Jefferson would feel about the world he did not live to see—in particular the America of our time.

Of Most Concern

The list is long. He'd be very much concerned about the magnitude of the national debt and the apparent indifference of the American people to what for him would be a fundamental issue. He would be aghast that the United States is now a world military and industrial empire. He would be surprised and alarmed by the size, the scope, and the social penetration of the national governmental.

He would be deeply troubled by the national security state: the seventeen intelligence-gathering agencies, including the CIA, the FBI, the NSC, etc.

He would be distressed by the seeming indifference of the American people to the loss of their republic, if by republic we mean severely limited government.

He would shake his head at the mediocrity of our educational system, and wonder what we are doing for thirteen years with young people if we don't teach them to read well, do sums, write clearly, and develop critical thinking skills.

He would be deeply concerned about the role of big money in our political process. He would be alarmed by the power of social media, especially its power to engage in character assassination, anonymous innuendo, and pronouncements that appear in public without any check or restraining mechanism whatsoever.

He would lament the loss of civility in American life, the rise of a number of strains of vulgarity, rudeness, and salaciousness, the collapse of respect and the viciousness of the partisanship of our time. He would be flabbergasted by pornography, cyber-pornography, soft pornography, and the general sexualization of American culture.

On the other hand, he would be thrilled by the electronification of information, the vast number of books now available in free electronic form, and the methods of communication now available to virtually every American. He would, of course, have the best smart phones available, the best laptop computer, and Fitbits of every sort.

He would marvel at modern medicine, which might have saved five of his children from premature death, and his wife, Martha, too. He would be thrilled by space, oceanic, and terrestrial exploration.

He would order the best wines from Napa Valley (using liberal credit lines) and perhaps even some Virginia wines.

Supreme Court

Jefferson believed in legislative supremacy. He had serious distrust of the federal judiciary, partly on constitutional principle but also because he realized that the judiciary had become the last fortress of the Federalist Party. He would be appalled by the idea that—in our time—nine unelected and essentially unimpeachable persons can determine the destiny of a third of a billion people.

Jefferson wanted the judiciary to be somewhat independent of the American voter, but not too independent of what he called the decided will of the American people. Jefferson's concept of the Constitution's doctrine of checks and balances required that each of the three branches of the national government have the capacity to resist—or check—excesses in the other two, but he believed strongly that the legislative branch, because it was the one closest to the will of the people, should have slightly more power than the other two.

The recent politicization of the Supreme Court would certainly worry Jefferson, who believed that the only way the system would work was when the justices were high-minded, conservative, and nonpartisan individuals who merely wanted to be faithful to the Constitution and especially the Bill of Rights. At the same time, the three men Jefferson appointed to the high court were all chosen to reinforce his own views of the Constitution and America's destiny.

Jefferson's ideal would be strict constructionists who tried to adhere as completely as possible to the explicit intent of the Founding Fathers. He was opposed to broad construction of the Constitution or implied powers. At the same time, however, he believed that we should tear up the Constitution from time to time, perhaps as often as every nineteen years. In short, Jefferson was in favor of a sequence of constitutions that would be strictly interpreted during their time of validity, and then replaced, once per generation, by another strictly-construed constitution.

We know this much for sure. Jefferson was passionately antagonistic to his distant cousin John Marshall, great chief justice of the Supreme Court who presided over that branch of government for thirty-four years.

Presidential Power

Jefferson favored a weak executive. Like others who grew up

under what they took to be the despotism of British monarchy, and because he had a principled commitment to legislative supremacy, Jefferson would be deeply alarmed by the power now held by American presidents and their administrative aides. Jefferson believed that power is dangerous when concentrated in the hands of the few or in the hands of one, safer when diffused—his word— among as many individuals or entities as practicable. He believed in the clarifying and distilling power of majority rule, where good sense could argue against nonsense, and every idea would be refined by debate and sustained scrutiny.

The modern presidency is so powerful that it effectively negates the intentions of the founders. Jefferson was a good enough student of history to realize that as America ceased to be a republic and became a continental empire, the original Constitution might not any longer manage public affairs well or efficiently. That's why he advocated tearing up the Constitution every generation, and writing a new constitution better suited to the actual needs and conditions of the new era. In other words, he would probably prefer a revised constitution that recognized the executive needs of a world that works by the speed of sound rather than the three-mile-per-hour world he lived in. That might grant the executive more power than Jefferson the republican was comfortable with, but it would permit the new constitutional fathers and mothers to find the balance between giving the executive much of the power it needs to function in the twenty-first century and also hemming it in with intelligent and enforceable restraints.

The situation as it has developed is nearly the worst of all possible worlds for Jefferson. The modern president has enormous and largely unchecked power, and yet we continue to pretend that a constitution written before steam power or hygiene or the immune system was understood can somehow be made to fit conditions essentially alien to the Founding Fathers.

Above all, Jefferson believed that matters of war and taxation must begin in the House of Representatives, because that is the branch closest to the sovereign, the people, and they must be consulted as directly as possible on questions of that gravity and magnitude.

Gerrymandering

The term gerrymandering dates from Jefferson's time, in honor of the eccentric Elbridge Gerry of Massachusetts, who benefited from an electoral district so distorted that it resembled a salamander. Presumably, given our capacity today to use computers to create rigorously fair and competitive districts, Jefferson would be in favor of taking legislative districting out of the hands of politicians and letting demographic engineers carve up the nation's geography.

In his own time Jefferson was in favor of voter suppression. He believed that women should not vote or hold public office. He did not consider Native Americans citizens of the United States because they were part of a distinct national sovereignty. As a slaveholder he did not favor giving enslaved people the right to vote, and at no point did he indicate support for the voting rights of free black Americans. It is true that Jefferson was an advocate of universal white manhood suffrage, at a time when that was regarded by many as a dangerously radical idea.

It seems likely that if Jefferson were alive today, he would oppose any sort of voter suppression, candid or by way of subterfuge.

Presidential Immunity

Like most of the Founding Fathers, Jefferson believed we needed to put into public office only men (always men) of great personal and public virtue. He probably would favor the Justice Department's protocol of not permitting the indictment of sitting presidents on the principle that the work of the executive is too important to distract with what could be judicial harassment and nuisance suits. For Jefferson, the proper remedy for presidential misconduct was impeachment. He probably would have favored a wider definition of impeachment than the one chosen by the Founding Fathers in Philadelphia. (He was in France at the time of the Constitutional Convention). Jefferson also understood that our quadrennial presidential elections give the people a superb tool for retiring a bad, mediocre, or abusive president (or other national officer).

I feel certain that Jefferson would favor prosecution of former executives for crimes committed in office, but not crimes involving executive policy. In the batture case that plagued him in his retirement, Jefferson argued that a president should not be sued by individuals or entities for his official actions during or after his time in office.

Healthcare

Jefferson was openly suspicious of the medicine of his time. He certainly would not have believed that the government of the United States could be trusted to manage the health of its citizens. For Jefferson, almost everything in life was a private, not a public, matter. He saw the national government as little more than a national referee. Proactive government of the kind we now accept would have appalled him.

However, Jefferson believed that whenever the national government is involved in any aspect of American life, it must dedicate itself to equal access for all. In other words, for Jefferson, the national government should either stay out of the healthcare world altogether (his preference) or—if it were involved—it needs to make sure that it is not serving some of the American people better than others. Even before the Affordable Care Act, our national government was involved in healthcare research, funding, and delivery in a myriad of ways. That means—according to Jefferson's concept of distributive justice—that the national government must make sure that some Americans are not served by that investment more than others, or at the expense of others. Jefferson's preferred national healthcare plan? Stay healthy.

Pro-Choice or Pro-Life

Jefferson would not want to talk about this profoundly personal matter. I'm guessing that Jefferson would regard abortion as a matter between a woman and her husband, a woman and her physician, and a woman and her pastor, but not between a woman and her government. There were abortions in Jefferson's time, though not surgical abortions. This is such a divisive issue that I hesitate to address it at all. Still, it is hard to think that Thomas Jefferson could ever be convinced that the government of the United States would pay for any abortion for any reason at any time.

Artist: John Trumbull (1788)
The Thomas Jefferson Foundation

This image of Jefferson was copied by John Trumbull from his monumental painting The Declaration of Independence. Jefferson was 33 years old when he wrote the Declaration. Trumbull, born in Connecticut, met Jefferson in London in 1786, accepted Jefferson's invitation to visit him for a time in his diplomatic quarters in Paris, where he could finish the monumental painting with advice from that monumental event's principal eye witness. This painting, drawn from the epic canvas, was completed in 1788. It was Trumbull who introduced Jefferson to Richard and Maria Cosway.

Mather Brown's portrait of Jefferson was the first ever made of the future president. Jefferson was in Britain at the time (1786). He was 43 years old. Brown's Jefferson wears a wig and elegant, frilled clothing. Brown was a Massachusetts-born American artist who was mastering his craft under the care of the painter Benjamin West. The painting was made for John and Abigail Adams. Jefferson would not have allowed himself to be seen in such courtly clothing in the United States.

Artist: Rembrandt Peale (1805)
The Thomas Jefferson Foundation

Jefferson's friend Charles Willson Peale painted this portrait of America's first Secretary of State in 1791, just two years after Jefferson returned from France. Jefferson was 48 years old at the time. Peale created a series of paintings of American worthies for his gallery and museum in Philadelphia. Peale also painted Meriwether Lewis and William Clark. Jefferson was an increasingly unhappy member of President Washington's cabinet, but he took great joy in participating in the enlightened cultural world of Philadelphia.

Gilbert Stuart made three images of Thomas Jefferson. The first was in 1800. Jefferson paid Stuart $100 for the portrait but could not persuade Stuart to deliver it to him. In the spring of 1805 Stuart painted this image of Jefferson at his studio in Washington, DC. Known as the Edgehill painting, this is one of the best portraits ever made of Jefferson, but once again Jefferson could not get Stuart to present it to him. Eventually, in 1821, when Jefferson was approaching death, Stuart delivered up two of his portraits, the 1805 Medallion and one of the other two. Even Jefferson's Monticello is not sure which one.

Gilbert Stuart painted this Medallion portrait of Jefferson in 1805. It depicts Jefferson in the manner of a classical hero. Jefferson's granddaughter Ellen Coolidge called the Medallion "an incomparable portrait, and the only likeness ever taken of him I think that gives a good idea of the original." Jefferson was able to wrest this painting out of the hands of Stuart, who was never quite satisfied that he had finished his paintings, and who got into a mild misunderstanding with Jefferson about who had paid for what and who really owned the paintings.

Artist: Thomas Sully (1821)
The Thomas Jefferson Foundation

Thomas Sully's full-length portrait of Jefferson was painted in 1821 when Jefferson was 78 years old. Sully had been commissioned to paint a portrait of Jefferson for the US Military Academy at West Point. Jefferson sat for the artist off and on for twelve days at Monticello. One version of this painting was purchased by Jefferson's protégé and "adoptive son" William Short, and presented to the American Philosophical Society, of which Jefferson was the president for eighteen years.

Q&A with Clay

During my many lectures and public performances as Thomas Jefferson, I welcome questions from moderators and spectators. Some come from a perspective of gentle curiosity and others with fury over seeming contradictions in Jefferson's character. Many citizens want to know how the third US president might view current issues of a world that, to him, would be barely recognizable. Below are some of the questions I am most often asked, and an attempt in few words to address them.

I've heard you say we are no longer a republic? Why?

A republic is a place of self-reliant individuals with a severely limited government. I could stop there. You cannot have hundreds of military bases around the globe and be a republic. You cannot have the Koch brothers and scores of other individuals of vast wealth buying influence and be a republic. You cannot have the obscene wealth and income gap between the tiny handful of super-rich in America and the rest of the population and be a republic. You cannot be a superpower—or, worse, the world's unipower—and be a republic. You cannot be a nation of consumers but not engaged citizens and be a republic. And so on. We are a semi-benign global empire pretending to be a republic. If we were a republic, the citizens of the United States would be in the streets demanding change. Instead, they are in their homes watching reality TV shows.

Is there anything like a Jeffersonian party or movement in the United States?

Unfortunately, no. We see glimpses and glimmers. There are hundreds of thousands, perhaps millions, of Jeffersonians around the United States, but they have nowhere to direct their aspirations and their energies. I think most people used to have the sense that the Democratic Party was somehow the heir to Jefferson's vision, but surely Jefferson would not find much to admire in the welfare state, in a world of swollen government programs, and runaway debt. It all depends on what part of Jefferson you choose to emphasize. If you are most drawn to his notions of a severely limited government, you may wind up with the Freedom Caucus, the Tea Party, and the Libertarians. Otherwise, you are likely to hold your nose and vote for the Democrats, because they share Jefferson's view that education is the answer and the belief that there has to be some measurable equality among American citizens.

But no true Jeffersonian can be happy with either of the existing political parties. And now the word *Jefferson* has lost some, perhaps much, of its luster, because Jefferson was a slaveholder, a racist, and the master of Sally Hemings. My point—passionately held—is that we need the *Jeffersonian* even if we wish to distance ourselves from *Jefferson*. That's why I search for other monikers: Second American Enlightenment, New Enlightenment, a New Agrarianism, etc. We need either a grassroots movement that begins with a program not unlike the principles articulated in this book, or a very wealthy Bloomberg-Buffett type who embodies these values to create a new third-party infrastructure. Better the former than the latter. It's not Jeffersonian from the top down.

Can we become a republic again?

I'm not sure. It seems pretty unlikely. We had our chance, but then we let it slip away. It is possible that the end of the American republic was inevitable, given the larger global dynamics of modernity. But we can probably be a little more like a republic again. We'd have to find a way to take money out of the political system (I have thoughts about that), balance the budget and pay off the national debt, pull back dramatically from our military presence in the rest of the world, start eliminating one unnecessary government program and department after the next, accept term limits, and wean nearly everyone off of the "welfare" rolls, including the rich and the middle class. We could do this, but oh my how millions would howl. There is no easy path.

More to the point, we'd have to recommit ourselves to constitutionalism. That would mean reining in the executive branch, making sure the war powers returned to the House of Representatives where they belong, and preventing the executive from committing troops anywhere in the world without a clear legislative authorization. We'd have to eliminate most executive orders. We'd need much more swift, clear, and severe conflict-of-interest protocols, and we'd have to flush out all corruptionists, time-servers, flatterers, dead weight, cronyists, stock-jobbers, and every complacent government officer from Congress, the executive, and the federal bureaucracy. We'd need to clear the House and Senate of those who are the lackeys of rich individuals and corporations. We'd have to prohibit any former member of Congress from lobbying or accepting positions on corporate boards. We'd have to be willing to impeach judges, justices, cabinet officials, and the president and vice president when they exceed their authority, violate the Constitution, or break the laws of the United States. We would need to rededicate ourselves in a serious, even fundamentalist way to John Adams' principle: "We are a nation of laws and not of men."

We would need to create mandatory civics and ethics courses in all publicly funded institutions—teaching every American the Constitution, the Bill of Rights, the Declaration of Independence, the UN Universal Declaration of Rights, the Geneva Conventions, and more; requiring every high school and college graduate to pass the same citizenship test we impose on immigrants to the United States.

We would need to institute mandatory national service for all young people, to be fulfilled for eighteen months between the seventeenth and twenty-fifth birthday.

Are you ready to roll up your sleeves?

How can we reconcile Jefferson being a slave owner while espousing a nation built on equality?

When you first encounter Jefferson—his inventiveness, his home, his elegance, his exquisite writings, his lovely vision of an agrarian republic—you feel deeply inspired. He's America's Leonardo da Vinci. You can hardly believe that such a man existed at the time of the American Revolution. You want to live in his republic. It's so instantly attractive. And then you have to face the problem of race and slavery in Jefferson. How could the man who wrote "All men are born equal" find a way to live, as Abraham Lincoln put it, by "wringing . . . bread from the sweat of other men's faces"?

At that point you learn two things: first, that Jefferson's explanations of this fundamental paradox are on the whole pretty weak and self-serving; second, that Jefferson seemed to live with this hypocrisy, this systematic form of human oppression, without much psychological fallout. Now add Sally Hemings to the story. This from a man who wrote that he abhorred race mixing. Even if you withhold judgment and merely try to understand how Jefferson could live with this whopping contradiction, you wind up shaking your head in disbelief. So, maybe all that talk about liberty and the rights of man was just rhetoric.

Once you have absorbed the unavoidable truth about Jefferson and race, you can never quite think of him in the same way again. He has lost permanent ground. The old view—dominant between 1939 and 1973—that Jefferson was a kind of sad, accidental, trapped but essentially benevolent slaveholder is actually just nonsense, and yet it was once national orthodoxy.

Add to this Jefferson's willing, sometimes ruthless, displacement of Native Americans, whom he ennobled in his writings and removed in his policies, and you really begin to wonder about the gap between what Jefferson wrote about human freedom and sovereignty and what he actually did in his life as a plantation owner, governor of Virginia, and president of the United States.

There is more. You learn that Jefferson was not as high-minded, serene, and above the fray as he wants you to believe from his exquisite Virgilian paeans to the garden world of "our own dear Monticello," where the sordid business of politics was not permitted to penetrate. The fact is that at certain times in his life Jefferson behaved like a take-no-prisoners political operative, that he fought hard, sometimes unscrupulously, to damage or destroy his enemies and win the fight for America—all the while panting for retirement and sighing about how unfitted he was for the rough business of politics, because he was at his core a man who lived only for his books, his gardens, and harmony. To paraphrase John Marshall, the morals of the man who paid James Callender to write dirt on John Adams were not those of a mild-mannered agrarian philosopher.

If you are anything like me, you cling to your paradigm of Jefferson as mild philosopher prince and reluctant slaveholder as long as possible, offering him benefit of the doubt again and again, but with a growing sense of uneasiness—until finally, one day, you wake up and the spell is broken. Now you see Jefferson as an agrarian poseur, a racist, bankrupt, an apartheidist, a Machiavellian politician, a two-faced backbiter, an unreliable friend, and a contemptible hypocrite.

At this point you have become an Adamsite, and you are not sure you want anything more to do with Thomas Jefferson. I have been an Adamsite several times in the course of my long affair with Jefferson, and I have had to struggle to work through it and recover. Ah, but we must learn from John Adams, Jefferson's most honest, unrelenting, and ultimately most loving friend. Adams became disillusioned with Jefferson sometime around 1789, and it just got worse and worse until 1800, when he realized that Jefferson was, in some important political respects, not an honorable man. The two great men last saw each other in the unfinished White House on one of the first days of March 1801. Adams, disgusted, dejected, and broken by personal loss, left town at dawn on March 4, 1801, to avoid being present at

Jefferson's inaugural. That hurt and angered Jefferson, who believed Adams' duty to the "peaceful transfer of power" required his presence at the first significant change of administrations in American history.

The two great men would have died unreconciled had it not been for the intervention of their mutual friend Dr. Benjamin Rush of Philadelphia. Neither elder statesman wanted to make the first move, but when Adams realized that Jefferson would not reject his overture, he blurted out, "I always loved Jefferson, and still love him." Adams found a way to work through his disillusionment, to forgive Jefferson as we forgive "our trespassers," and to find, on balance, much still to admire in his problematic friend from Virginia. Before he wound up dying simultaneously with Jefferson on July 4, 1826, Adams came to love Jefferson with a deeper, but somewhat shadowed, love, and he approved of the Sage of Monticello even if he could not always approve of Jefferson's public actions in a fallen world.

Anyone who loves Jefferson over a long period of time goes through these phases. Some people cannot get beyond slavery, or the dispossession of Indian tribes, or Jefferson's political ruthlessness, or—to sum it all up—his hypocrisy, and they transfer their admiration to Alexander Hamilton. To that, all I can say is good luck with your dreams of a republic. It is much better to work hard like John Adams to find a way to love Jefferson warts and all. And if you can, the payoff is extraordinary: his taste, his capacity for friendship, his whimsical life as a gardener, his love of great books, his outstanding clarity of expression, his usual high-mindedness, his deep devotion to the American project, and his belief that the people are up to the challenge of governing themselves with good sense and dignity.

So, an Adamsite is first someone who has to break with Jefferson because the pain of his hypocrisies is too great to bear; then later that same person finds a way to admire Jefferson again in a big, almost overwhelming way, but never with quite the same "innocence." The honeymoon is over.

How much does Jefferson's complicity in slavery bother you, personally?

I'm deeply troubled by it. We can say he was a man of his times, that we should not judge figures of the past by the standards (or perceptions) of the present, that we need to apply the "whole man theory," etc. But, in the end, the individual who wrote that "all men are created equal" owned as many as 600 other human beings, and bought and sold them, too. Hunted them down when they escaped. There is really no defense of this. Jefferson, Washington, Madison, Patrick Henry, and others among the Founding Fathers constantly lamented that they were being "enslaved" by the British king and parliament. Think of the irony of that. In actual fact, they were being taxed without real representation, but nobody was kidnapping them, packing them in the stinking holds of ships, selling them in chains to men who inspected their calves and teeth, whipping them for wanting to be free or resisting their enslavement, breeding them for profit, or raping their women at will.

I know this sounds horrible, but about once every six weeks I reach the very brink of the continental divide, on the other side of which I know that I have to quit representing Thomas Jefferson or taking him seriously as a great man. I get right to the brink of that divide, and I realize that I would be much more consistent with my core value system if I just divorced Jefferson once and for all and said, "There are things I love about Jefferson, lots of them, but I just cannot any longer in good conscience tie my life to someone who found a way to live cheerfully with slavery." I linger there for a few hours or a few days. And then I turn myself around and find a way. Thomas Jefferson is that great. He is that magnificent. He is that right about America. And he represents what I admire in life on earth so wonderfully in so many ways. Like so many others, I have to find a way to accept Jefferson, warts and all, without becoming complacent about the unfinished agenda of the American experiment.

But the time in which slavery was a kind of asterisk in Jefferson's story (the twentieth century) is over, once and for all.

So, you still considered yourself a Jeffersonian?

Yes, without question. I want the United States to be the noblest, most idealistic, most enlightened nation on earth. I want the American people to be the best-educated, freest, most self-actualized people on earth, and if we are not number one in the most important categories (that can be a bit jingoistic), then to be always in the cluster of most enlightened nations. I want every other country to look on us with admiration and envy. I want us to try to set the gold standard for life on earth. I want the American people to be self-reliant, resourceful, thoughtful, humane, civil, quirky, and wonderfully creative.

What good is it to be a Jeffersonian if the larger culture is in steep decline?

Whatever else is wrong with America, it allows an enormous amount of freedom in our choice of lifestyles. I wish there were tens of millions of Jeffersonians in the United States, beginning with our presidents, but if you want to be an exemplar of the Enlightenment in a vast sea of Hamiltonians, Jacksonians, or reality TV addicts, nobody will get in your way. Thanks to social media, you can find each other and create virtual salons, even if you cannot muster a quorum for the physical version. If you are or become a Jeffersonian, people around you will notice. Some of them will be inspired by your example. We all want to live in the society of our dreams and ideals, but each of us only gets one life, and it is important that we use what time we have to try to embody the values that matter most to us. Better to be a relatively lonely Jeffersonian than part of the herd at the bear baiting or a slavering cypher in the angry mob.

Besides, there is nothing wrong with a life of wine, books, conversation, travel, friendship, manners, and curiosity! This may be the twenty-first century's answer to Voltaire's Candide, who for a long time gave the life project his all, but eventually withdrew to tend his garden in a completely private manner. Almost no Jeffersonian is entirely alone thanks to our astounding global connectivity.

How do you know you understand Jefferson and are true to his vision?

Well, Jefferson himself would probably say you should read his letters and a handful of biographies and decide for yourself. Which is what I say, too. We know what Jefferson did not want: a strong central national government; heavy taxation; world empire; a welfare state; a largely ignorant public.

He did not want the United States to be the policeman of the world. He did not want the American people to congregate in cities. He did not want a swollen national debt. He did not want the national government to swallow up the states. He did not want American citizens to be dependent on entities they could not control for their basic needs. He did not want career politicians, a large permanent bureaucracy, intrusive regulation, broad construction of the Constitution, or foreign interventionism. We know those things with certainty.

Fortunately, Jefferson was forthright about his vision of America. He preserved his documents, including his 22,000 letters. We have his annual messages to Congress and his two inaugural addresses. We have his "confession of faith" in *Notes on the State of Virginia*.

There is plenty to debate. I'm still trying to finish a big book called *The Paradox of Thomas Jefferson*. Nobody has been able to make sense of Jefferson's inconsistencies and what might be called Jeffersonian silences. I don't pretend that my understanding of Jefferson is the only right one. But I am pretty sure I have distilled his outlook, his character, his personality, and his vision accurately after years of hard reading, hard thinking, and constant conversation and performance. I'm not one of Jefferson's diehard defenders—on slavery, on Sally Hemings, on the displacement of Native Americans, on his political maneuverings, or on his occasional abuse of civil liberties. I don't believe I am in denial about any of Jefferson's darker views or deeds.

But I am certainly not one of his hardline detractors. In my view, there is much more good in Jefferson than bad. It would be a fatal mistake to our civilization to scrape Jefferson off Mount Rushmore because he does not conform to our standards of justice and integrity. At the same time, it would be a mistake not to cast a shadow onto his visage at Mount Rushmore, and a darker shadow onto the Jefferson Memorial because it quotes him out of context in a way that protects memorial visitors from what is problematic in his character and achievement.

I've tried to be scrupulously honest about Jefferson and Jeffersonians in this book. At times I have had to articulate views that are not my own as I try to project Jefferson into our time. He's not a twenty-first-century liberal. But he's not a twenty-first-century libertarian either. A number of years ago, I gave a Jefferson performance at a US Senate retreat in rural Pennsylvania. Afterwards, Senator Joe Biden came up to congratulate me. But he said, "You know, Jefferson is closer to Pat Buchanan than he is to the modern Democratic Party. We've evolved." In many respects Jefferson is closer to the Tea Party and the Freedom Caucus than to the Democrats. He could not be a modern Republican, because he would not align himself with the party of wealth.

Why do you choose to live in North Dakota?

Everyone's from somewhere. I grew up on the plains of North Dakota. At one time North Dakota was one of the most Jeffersonian places in America. It was, twenty-five years ago, a family farm state with a very wide middle (middling) class, with very few rich and even fewer poor. It was, and is, a state of decent, hard-working, self-reliant, modest people who play by the rules and take pride in their practical mastery of life. I love North Dakota with all my heart. In fact, I'm just finishing a new book on the future of North Dakota. The working title is *So Who Are We Now?* though that is unlikely to be the final title of the study.

Jefferson bought much of North Dakota from Napoleon in 1803. In other words, one white man who never got anywhere near

North Dakota bought much of the state from another white man who never visited the New World! Nobody consulted the Mandan, Hidatsa, Arikara, Lakota, Assiniboine, Dakota, or Ojibwe, the actual sovereigns of the Upper Missouri, as 575 million acres changed hands from the French to the upstart Americans. No wonder Native Americans live their lives in barely-modulated rage. And if you followed the Dakota Access Pipeline debacle of 2017, you know things haven't really changed very much.

One of my passions is spirit of place. How does a landscape shape human character? Does it matter whether you grow up in Idaho as opposed to Las Vegas, in Versailles (pronounced Ver-sales), Kentucky, as opposed to Versailles in France? One of the truisms of sociology is "Where you stand depends on where you sit." Does where you call home help to determine your outlook on life, your politics, your idea of America? I'm honored to call myself a North Dakotan. I could live anywhere, but I choose to live here. At this point, I wish North Dakota were a little less red, but I don't wish it were blue.

Jefferson believed that farmers are the chosen people of God. I share that view, however corny that sounds. North Dakota still requires every farm to be a family farm in some sense of that word. I like that. If you get out into the countryside and the small towns, you can still meet people shaped by the agrarian lifestyle.

You often emphasize the agrarian. Why is that so important in thinking about Jefferson?

I remember once meeting a really remarkable judge in Iowa who had read many biographies of Jefferson, had fascinating hobbies, wrote poetry, had a really good personal library, etc. We had dinner. He said, "I really love Jefferson and what he stands for—except for all that agrarian crap." I wanted to say, "Well, it actually all pivots on that 'agrarian crap,'" but I held my tongue. The key words for Jefferson are "nature," "natural law," "nature's God," and the sense you get is that these should be spelled with a capital *N*.

What is the core of Jefferson's vision? I have thought long and hard about this. It's a thought experiment. If you took "X" out of Jefferson, would he still be Jefferson? So, if you removed ancient Greek from the list of his accomplishments, would you still have Jefferson? Of course. How about paleontology? Yes, still Jefferson. How about slavery? Well, he'd be much poorer and would live less luxuriously, but oh my, he'd be one of the single greatest individuals who ever lived if he were not so deeply, perhaps fatally, compromised by slavery. What about architecture—what if he had lived in a typical Virginia planter's house? Well, we're getting closer to the core of the man now, but yes, he'd still mostly be Jefferson. How about wine? Jefferson said he could not live without wine, but we know that's not really true. He'd be sorry, but he'd still be Jefferson. And so on. Well then, what if you took the agrarian out of Jefferson?

He said a great thing about his love of growing things: "I have often thought that if heaven had given me choice of my position and calling, it should have been on a rich spot of earth, well-watered, and near a good market for the productions of the garden. No occupation is so delightful to me as the culture of the earth, and no culture comparable to that of the garden."[18] This should be the manifesto of all true gardeners. Jefferson's agrarianism had more to do with curiosity and experiment and the parable of the mustard seed than with producing commodities for the market.

I have some family farm in my background, though I have never had to earn my living from the productions of the earth. My grandparents were dairy farmers in western Minnesota. My daughter, Catherine Missouri, grew up in 4-H, which I regard as more important to her formation than the K–12 school curriculum. We have reached the terminus of gigantic industrial agriculture. It is mighty productive, and it has solved the problem of famine, but it is not a sustainable way to grow food or live in something like harmony

---

18   To Charles Willson Peale, August 20, 1811

on and with the good earth. I see the breakdown and breakup of that paradigm in the later twenty-first century. My hope is that we turn to a higher Jeffersonian agrarianism, with an emphasis on the *culture* in agriculture. Jefferson believed that a free and virtuous man (human) is someone with his or her hands in the soil.

At any rate, I think you can take a number of elements and avocations and attributes out of Jefferson and still have Jefferson, but you cannot cut him off from his life with the earth and nature and still have Jefferson. That's the center of his soul and his vision for America.

What's your dream for the next decade of your life?

I want to get a camper rig not unlike Steinbeck's *Rocinante* and go in search of America. Actually, I have dreamed of doing this since I was fourteen, but now I have purpose. Then it was wanderlust. When I get out into the country, into the heart of it, I always cheer up. I want to go find the Jeffersonians—the Renaissance men and women who are scattered across our landscape, doing remarkable things in the humanities, in the arts, in science, in public life. I want to go to all the national parks and a wide range of historic sites, follow along with Lewis and Clark again—one of my particular scholarly interests— and seek out sites relating to each of my favorite historical characters. Breathe in the continent, and try to assess where we are when we turn away from major media and try to live our lives in whatever's left of the American republic. I want to call in the Jefferson Hour from the road, post photo essays and video interviews and commentary, and write a book about a Jeffersonian's search for the heart of America in the third decade of the twenty-first century. I want to sleep among the redwoods, in the Grand Canyon, in a cypress swamp, in Indian country, in nearly nameless mountain ranges in Montana, near the source of the Mississippi and the Colorado and the Ohio Rivers, in the parking lots of presidential libraries, but also where Crazy Horse was cut down and where Chief Joseph surrendered, at Walden Pond, and at stations of the Underground Railroad. I believe my whole life to this point has been a preparation for this journey, and I plan to come back with a book worth reading ready for the press.

What, in a nutshell, is the Enlightenment?

Reason, reform, rationality. A belief in human progress, science, and (for many) the perfectibility of man. Taxonomy: classification of plants, animals, minerals; the periodic table; library classification systems; the varieties of humankind; the constituents of the air; classification of the world's languages. Encyclopedias, almanacs, and digests of knowledge. Separation of church and state. The rights of man. *The Rights of Man.*

Coffeehouses, salons, and the second great age of exploration. Captain Cook in Tahiti to observe the Transit of Venus. Benjamin Franklin seeking to protect Cook from naval interference during the war with Britain. Alexander von Humboldt detouring to America to meet the great Jefferson and get his copy of *Notes on Virginia* signed. Dr. Johnson's *Dictionary of the English Language.* The invention of the Noble Savage. The termination of biblical literalism and the quest for the historical Jesus. Penal reform. The birth of the magazine. *Robinson Crusoe* and *Gulliver's Travels.* The birth of geology. The Longitude Prize. Herschel's discovery of Uranus. The belief that behind every phenomenon there is a simple law of gravity that we need only discern and then apply by way of reform.

What do you mean by the *Jefferson Music*?

To put it in a nutshell, it's Jefferson's ability to write things so compelling and lyrical and beautiful and aspirational that they make you ache. Nobody in American history ever sang the song of America as Jefferson does. Nobody ever made this country and its people feel more beautiful and noble in our republican experiment than did Jefferson. He understood what all successful presidents have understood—that if you want to lead this country, you have to sing the Song of America.

And he meant it. He meant all those poetic and magnificent things he wrote: "Nothing is more certainly written in the book of fate, than these people are to be free." "The god who gave us life gave us liberty at the same time: the hand of force may destroy, but cannot disjoin them." "A rising nation, spread over a wide and fruitful land, traversing all the seas with the rich productions of their industry, engaged in commerce with nations who feel power and forget right, advancing rapidly to destinies beyond the reach of mortal eye." "I know no safe depository of the ultimate powers of the society but the people themselves; and if we think them not enlightened enough to exercise their control with a wholesome discretion, the remedy is not to take it from them, but to inform their discretion by education. This is the true corrective of abuses of constitutional power."[19] And so on. Ad infinitum. Jefferson was the poet of the American dream.

Alexander Pope defined wit as "what oft was thought but never so well expressed." Jefferson expressed the core catechism of American life, including the American dream, so beautifully that from time to time we delude ourselves into believing that we can actually live in that republic. I do actually believe we can. Even now, after thirty years of marriage to Thomas Jefferson.

I remember once reading a passage by James Madison on the virtue of the agrarian lifestyle. Even in that summary I have been more poetic than Madison was in describing the importance of agriculture to our national character and independence. Madison understood the doctrine. In many respects he was a better thinker and statesman than Jefferson. But Madison did not have the Jefferson Music. He was prosaic. He said what he said well, but he could not inspire, he could not lift, he could not make people yearn. Madison argued his point well, but it was mere prose. Then you turn to Jefferson: "Those who labor in the earth are the chosen people of God, if ever he had

19   Thomas Jefferson *Autobiography,* 1821; *A Summary View of the Rights of British America,* 1774; *First Inaugural Address,* March 4, 1801; to William Charles Jarvis, September 28, 1820.

a chosen people, whose breasts he has made his peculiar deposit for substantial and genuine virtue." Still, one problem of the Jefferson Music is that it lulls you to sleep. It is so compelling and so beautiful that you forget to examine the proposition through a rational lens. Jefferson describes a world you want to live in, but sometimes you forget to ask just how that world would work.

Why did Jefferson so dislike Hamilton? Political reasons?

Jefferson disliked Hamilton for a range of good reasons, and a couple of personal ones. Hamilton believed that war can be a source of national glory. Jefferson was a quasi-pacifist who believed that war should be the very last melancholy answer to conflicts that can be resolved in no other way. Hamilton wanted a strong national government and wanted to swallow up the idea of state sovereignty as much as possible. Jefferson's views were exactly the opposite. Hamilton is the creator of the national debt, which he believed an important tool of the national economy. Jefferson believed that a national debt is a national disgrace, a way of taxing our children and grandchildren without their consent. Hamilton wanted to interpret the Constitution flexibly and broadly so that it would not be a straitjacket that prevented a great nation from achieving its goals. Jefferson was a strict constructionist. Hamilton loved power and sought to use it. Jefferson was suspicious of power and sought to make the national government as mild and minimalist as possible. Hamilton tilted towards Great Britain, Jefferson towards France. Hamilton sought to create a mixed economy and to provide government support for infant industries. Jefferson was a thoroughgoing agrarian. Hamilton was a monarchist and an advocate of aristocracy. Jefferson was a republican who wanted to prevent an American class system. Shall I go on?

Jefferson also distrusted Hamilton because he was ambitious, driven, ruthless, a workaholic. Jefferson had a much more gentlemanly view of public service, and he presented himself as a man without significant ambition. And he was distressed that the great George Washington seemed to prefer Hamilton's policies to his own. Both Jefferson and Hamilton sought to be Washington's favorite, in some sense his adoptive son. Jefferson found it appalling that the general, a fellow Virginia planter and agrarian, generally sided with the upstart from the Caribbean.

How much did Jefferson love wine?

Just as Jefferson said he could not live without books, music, or friendship, he could not live without wine.

Jefferson drank a couple of glasses of the best wine he could afford every day of his adult life. And yet he was never intoxicated. He regarded wine as a health food, ideal if subtle medicine, and of course as liquid art. He did not regard it as an intoxicant. He read fine books while sipping fine wine and listening to fine music.

Jefferson preferred French wines, particularly Bordeaux. He did not anticipate the apotheosis of Napa Valley in California and the aesthetic revolution brought about by the remarkable Robert Mondavi (1913–2008). Because Jefferson believed that every person's first country is his own, but every rational person's second country must be France, he would even now prefer to purchase French wines whenever possible. As an American patriot, and boyish advocate of all things American, he could not now fail to prize the wines of California. Whether he would yet find enough to admire in Virginia wines is more problematic.

Jefferson was America's first great wine connoisseur. His short list: from Bordeaux, Lafite, Latour, Margaux, and especially Château Haut-Brion; Rhone's Hermitage; Volnay, Chambertin, and Montrachets from Burgundy; Tuscan reds; Sauternes.

When he discovered true wine (partly in Williamsburg, more emphatically during his five years in France), he ceased to enjoy what he called the fortified or "alcoholic wines," of the British empire— port, Madeira, sherry, and brandy. While in France (1784–89) he made a serious study of the French wine industry. He visited some of the best vineyards in France, got to know some of the growers and vignerons, found agents (*negotiantes*) to make purchases for him, and devised methods to ship wine from Bordeaux and Marseilles to the New World without damaging its delicate artistry in transit. He became the wine adviser to the other four of the first five presidents of the United States. Even his political enemies admired his taste in wine and his exquisite hospitality, at the White House and at Monticello.

Jefferson urged fellow travelers to drink *vin ordinaire* (i.e., house wine) when they traveled. If wine reinforces class hierarchy, Jefferson would be disappointed.

Jefferson's Bona Fides and Family Tree

J efferson was born April 13, 1743, in Shadwell, Virginia, and died July 4, 1826, at his Monticello home. He was the third of ten siblings and was raised on his father's plantation in Albemarle, Virginia. Both of his parents' families emigrated to America from the United Kingdom.

Jefferson was 6'2" with sandy colored hair, hazel eyes and freckles. His voice was husky but weak and stammering. He was obsessively private, avoided eye contact and was mostly silent when in public. He was reserved and even cold with new acquaintances. He avoided conflict, preferring not to confront in person, yet he clung stubbornly to his favorite ideas.

He suffered from periodic migraines, preferred vegetables to meat, and drank wine in moderation. Women saw him as charming, but not seductive.

Jefferson was tutored as a child, and formally educated at the College of William and Mary in Williamsburg. He had a vaunted political career that included stints as an elected legislator and then governor of Virginia. In the federal government, he was minister to France and then secretary of state under President George Washington. Jefferson served one term as America's vice president and two terms as president. He and colleagues formed a political association called the Democratic-Republican Party, which advocated for limiting the powers of the federal government and a farm-based society.

Jefferson was married once. The ceremony was held January 1, 1772, on a plantation near Williamsburg, Virginia. His wife, Martha Wayles Skelton, was the widow of a friend from the College of William and Mary in Williamsburg. Thomas and Martha were married ten years and had six children together. Four died in infancy. Two daughters lived to be adults; both married cousins and had children of their own.

Jefferson's relationship with family slave Sally Hemmings started five years after Martha's death. Sally was thirty years younger than the widower Jefferson. Sally was born in 1773 and was part of Martha's inheritance from her father. Sally came to Jefferson's estate as an infant, along with her siblings and her mother.

It is most probable that Sally was a half-sister of Martha, both women sharing the same father, John Wayles. Her mother was Beth Hemmings, a mixed-race woman who was one of Wayles' slaves. Sally was described as very attractive with straight black hair and light-colored skin. She was counted as white in the 1833 census. Jefferson never married Sally, but DNA testing and historical evidence strongly suggest they had six children together, two of whom died in infancy.

Jefferson and Martha's children
Martha (1772–1836)
Jane Randolph (1774–75)
Unnamed son (1777)
Maria (1778–1804)
Lucy Elizabeth I (1780–81)
Lucy Elizabeth II (1782–84)

Sally Heming's children
Beverly (born 1798)
Harriet (born 1801)
Madison (1805–1878)
Eston (1808–1853)

A Guide to Being Jeffersonian

Core Qualities

You don't have to do everything in this book to be Jeffersonian. Jefferson believed in human freedom, and he certainly did not hold himself up as the epitome of human enlightenment. It would be great if all of us tended vegetable gardens and read Homer in the original Greek, but as John Adams might say, we live in the real world.

The core qualities of a Jeffersonian are 1) an open, curious, seeking mind; 2) modesty and civility; 3) a life of reading, writing (if only letter writing), reflection, and engagement in nature; 4) a strong belief that humans are up to the challenge of governing themselves; 5) belief that reason is our only oracle.

The rest? Well, everybody's taste is different (*de gustibus non est disputandum*), and Jefferson himself said that if all visages and body types were identical, the world would be a very dreary place. So, too, with lifestyles, avocations, and passions.

The goal is to try to be a "woman for all seasons" but, meanwhile, to embody as many Jeffersonian traits and ideals as possible. And to never stop growing.

Good Citizenship

If you believe you can be a Jeffersonian citizen by paying your taxes, voting, and writing your congressman from time to time, you are not a Jeffersonian. To borrow from Theodore Roosevelt, you cannot be a true republican citizen without getting into the arena from time to time. You don't have to run for school board, but you had better attend their meetings.

Behavior

Think before you speak. Weigh your words carefully. Be more civil than those around you deserve. Trust science. Read, read, read. Write actual letters, even if they are electronic. Write down excerpts from the books that help you understand the world. Seek moderation in all things. Never pretend to know what you don't know. Avoid intoxication. Get outside and listen to the dictates of nature. Aspire to be rational. Avoid all righteousness. Seek out other people who share your commitment to reason, civility, and playful argument. Try to see things from the point of view of people you disagree with. Disagree as rational friends. Seek and preach harmony. Self-actualize in every way possible. Engage.

What to Read

Here are ten books to read: *Plutarch's Lives* of Julius Caesar, Brutus, Cicero, Solon, Lycurgus, Antony, and Cincinnatus. Michael Pollan's *The Omnivore's Dilemma*. Wendell Berry, *The Unsettling of America*. Carl Sagan, *The Demon-Haunted World*. Bill Bryson's *A Short History of Nearly Everything*. Yuval Harari's *Homo Deus: A Brief History of Tomorrow*. Daniel Defoe, *Robinson Crusoe*. Steven Pinker, *Enlightenment Now: The Case for Reason, Science, Humanism, and Progress*. David Wooten, *The Invention of Science: A New History of the Scientific Revolution*. And Mark Edmundson, *The Heart of the Humanities: Reading, Writing, Teaching*. If you read all of these books in the next year, your life will reach a higher orbit.

Spreading the Word

One way to imbue excitement about Jeffersonian principles is to tell everyone you know about *The Thomas Jefferson Hour* that appears on many NPR-affiliated stations around the country. You can find the podcast at Jeffersonhour.com. That site also includes my weekly Jefferson Watch essays, an archive of programs from the past ten years, information about the cultural tours I lead, and much more. *The Thomas Jefferson Hour* has been around for about twenty years.

Here's how it works. The host, David Swenson, introduces a topic and interviews Thomas Jefferson for about forty minutes. We take questions and comments from people all over the country, even from abroad. I do my very best to represent Jefferson accurately and with as much detail as possible, but I also try carefully to project Mr. Jefferson into a world that he did not live to observe. This is a somewhat speculative art, but it is less speculative than you might think, because Jefferson was the most forward-thinking of the Founding Fathers, and his worldview (his position on most subjects) was formed early in life and it did not change much in the decades that followed.

The last third of the program is "out of character." In this segment, I break character and comment on Jefferson as a humanities scholar. This permits me to distance myself from some of Jefferson's pronouncements and views, and it allows me to provide contextual commentary on the world of Thomas Jefferson.

We do fifty-two fresh programs per year. Some of the programs focus exclusively on listener questions. Some are seasonal: we do a Christmas show, a Fourth of July program, a New Year's show, etc. Other programs focus on special themes: Jefferson and wine; Jefferson and Native Americans; Jefferson in France; Jefferson's grandchildren. About a quarter of the programs are entirely out of character. Sometimes we explore a subject that is easier to approach as a scholar than as a historical impersonator. Sometimes I interview historians and other authors. Sometimes we respond to listener questions that are put to me as the Jefferson scholar.

It's fun, entertaining, informative, and I hope insightful. My goal is to create a haven of clarity, civility, thoughtfulness, and enlightenment in a world increasingly damaged by noise, disputatiousness, disrespect, and naked partisanship. I don't expect all of our listeners to agree with Mr. Jefferson or with me, but I hope all of them recognize the essential fairness and goodwill of the program. To keep the program alive, we need money and plenty of it. We've done all of this with exceedingly limited funds. With the money we need to market the program properly, we could possibly really make a difference in America. We need about $150,000 per year for ten years. If we had it, I promise we would be able to help change the national conversation.

A Baker's Dozen of Jefferson's Letters

No exploration of the ideas of Jefferson can compete with his own stupendous mastery of English prose. I have written in this book about what I call the Jefferson Music. You are about to get a short Jefferson symphony here.

Jefferson was astonishingly clear and articulate. In fact, he is one of the most lucid writers in American history. The only other presidents who belong to the small club of great writers are Theodore Roosevelt (the *writingest* president), and Abraham Lincoln, who may be the greatest writer in American presidential history. Jefferson himself said that his biography could best be written by a sequential examination of his letters. He did not write treatises or op-ed pieces. Aside from a handful of remarkable state papers, including of course the Declaration of Independence, the only long-form writing project of Jefferson's life was *Notes on the State of Virginia*, which was immediately recognized as an American classic.

Choosing just a baker's dozen of Jefferson's letters is excruciating. It would be easier to choose fifty. Since this book is primarily about Jeffersonianism and *vision*, I have selected letters that give you a good and representative window on Jefferson's idea of America, of revolution, of citizenship, and of what he called "the illimitable freedom of the human mind."

I have removed from some of these letters passages that are merely topical, or extraneous to the central point he wished to make. I have also taken the liberty of regularizing some of Jefferson's idiosyncratic spellings. You can find the full text of each of these letters, and tens of thousands more, at the Library of Congress archive or in a range of other sources.

Before each letter I have provided a very brief personal introduction, but I have deliberately limited myself to no more than 250 words, mostly to let Jefferson be Jefferson, but also to prevent myself from burying the Sage of Monticello with my commentary.

To Martha Jefferson Randolph
New York, July 17, 1790

At this point Jefferson had two surviving children, both daughters, Maria (Polly) and Martha (Patsy). Martha's widowed father-in-law had recently married a much younger woman, Gabriella Harvie. Thomas Mann Randolph Sr. was fifty. She was seventeen. Martha and her husband, Thomas Mann Randolph Jr., were embarrassed by the unfitness of the match, displeased with Gabriella's personality, and—like good characters in a Jane Austen novel—concerned about who would inherit the estate when the moment came. What I love about this letter is Jefferson's understanding that stoic imperturbability is preferable to emotional volatility and that an attitude of righteousness is likely to make matters worse rather than better, and that we need to be forgiving of others' weaknesses, given the universality of human weakness.

My Dear Patsy,

I received two days ago yours of July 2. with Mr. Randolph's of July 3. Mine of the 11th. to Mr. Randolph will have informed you that I expect to set out from hence for Monticello about the 1st. of September. As this depends on the adjournment of Congress and they begin to be impatient, it is more probable I may set out sooner than later. However my letters will keep you better informed as the time approaches.—Colo. Randolph's marriage was to be expected. All his amusements depending on society, he cannot live alone. The settlement spoken of may be liable to objections in point of prudence and justice. However I hope it will not be the cause of any diminution of affection between him and Mr. Randolph and yourself. That cannot remedy the evil, and may make it a great deal worse. Besides your interests which might be injured by a misunderstanding be assured that your happiness would be infinitely affected. It would be a cankerworm corroding eternally on your minds. Therefore, my dear child, redouble your assiduities to keep the affections of Colo. Randolph and his lady (if he is to have one) in proportion as the difficulties increase. He is an excellent good man, to whose temper nothing can be objected but too much facility, too much milk. Avail yourself of this softness then to obtain his attachment. If the lady has anything difficult in her dispositions, avoid what is rough, and attach her good qualities to you. Consider what are otherwise as a bad stop in your harpsichord. Do not touch on it, but make yourself happy with the good ones. Every human being, my dear, must thus be viewed according to what it is good for, for none of us, no not one, is perfect; and were we to love none who had imperfections this world would be a desert for our love. All we can do is to make the best of our friends: love and cherish what is good in them, and keep out of the way of what is bad: but no more think of rejecting them for it than of throwing away a piece of music for a flat passage or two. Your situation will require peculiar attentions and respects to both parties. Let no proof be too much for either your patience or acquiescence. Be you, my dear, the link of love, union, and peace for the whole family. The world will give you the more credit for it in proportion to the difficulty of the task. And your own happiness will be the greater as you perceive that you promote that of others. Former acquaintance, and equality of age, will render it the easier for you to cultivate and gain the love of the lady. The mother too becomes a very necessary object of attentions. This marriage renders it doubtful with me whether it will be better to direct our overtures to Colo. R. or Mr. H. for a farm for Mr. Randolph. Mr. H. has a good tract of land on the other side Edgehill, and it may not be unadvisable to begin by buying out a dangerous neighbor. I wish Mr. Randolph could have him sounded to see if he will sell, and at what price; but sounded thro' such a channel as would excite no suspicion that it comes from Mr. Randolph or myself. Colo. Monroe would be a good and unsuspected hand, as he once thought of buying the same lands. Adieu my dear child. Present my warm attachment to Mr. Randolph.

Yours affectionately,

To Charles Bellini
Paris, September 30, 1785

Most of this remarkable letter is reprinted here. Jefferson spent five years in France (1784–89), first as a minister-at-large and eventually as the American minister to France (effectively, the ambassador). It was one of the happiest and most important periods of Jefferson's life. Although he was shocked and dismayed by how little monogamy seemed to matter in France, he fell in love with French music, French painting, French sculpture, French architecture, French conversation, and French politeness. Jefferson realized that the things he loved about France were the privileges of the wealthy and the well-born, but he nevertheless greatly appreciated French high culture. I'm intrigued by Jefferson's comparison of temperate France with the drunkenness and brutality of American manners. There is an interesting book on this subject by W. J. Rorabaugh, *The Alcoholic Republic: An American Tradition.*

Dear Sir,

Behold me at length on the vaunted scene of Europe! It is not necessary for your information that I should enter into details concerning it. But you are perhaps curious to know how this new scene has struck a savage of the mountains of America. Not advantageously I assure you. I find the general fate of humanity here most deplorable. The truth of Voltaire's observation offers itself perpetually, that every man here must be either the hammer or the anvil. It is a true picture of that country to which they say we shall pass hereafter, and where we are to see god and his angels in splendor, and crowds of the damned trampled under their feet. While the great mass of the people are thus suffering under physical and moral oppression, I have endeavored to examine more nearly the condition of the great, to appreciate the true value of the circumstances in their situation which dazzle the bulk of the spectators, and especially to compare it with that degree of happiness which is enjoyed in America by every class of people. Intrigues of love occupy the younger, and those of ambition the more elderly part of the great. Conjugal love having no existence among them, domestic happiness, of which that is the basis, is utterly unknown. In lieu of this are substituted pursuits which nourish and invigorate all our bad passions, and which offer only moments of extasy amidst days and months of restlessness and torment. Much, very much inferior this to the tranquil permanent felicity with which domestic society in America blesses most of its inhabitants, leaving them to follow steadily those pursuits which health and reason approve, and rendering truly delicious the intervals of these pursuits. In science, the mass of people is two centuries behind ours, their literati half a dozen years before us. Books, really good, acquire just reputation in that time, and so become known to us and communicate to us all their advances in knowledge. Is not this delay compensated by our being placed out of the reach of that swarm of nonsense which issues daily from a thousand presses and perishes almost in issuing? With respect to what are termed polite manners, without sacrificing too much the sincerity of language, I would wish [my] countrymen to adopt just so much of European politeness as to be ready [to] make all those little sacrifices of self which really render European manners amiable, and relieve society from the disagreeable scenes to which rudeness often exposes it. Here it seems that a man might pass a life without encountering a single rudeness. In the pleasures of the table they are far before us, because with good taste they unite temperance. They do not terminate the most sociable meals by transforming themselves into brutes. I have never yet seen a man drunk in France, even among the lowest of the people. Were I to proceed to tell you how much I enjoy their architecture, sculpture, painting, music, I should want words. It is in these arts they shine. The last of them particularly is an enjoyment, the deprivation of which with us cannot be calculated. I am almost ready to say it is the only thing which from my heart I envy them, and which in spite of all the authority of the decalogue I do covet.—But I am running on in an estimate of things infinitely better known to you than to me, and which will only serve to convince you that I have brought with me all the prejudices of country, habit and age. But whatever I may allow to be charged to me as prejudice, in every other instance, I have one sentiment at least founded on reality: it is that of the perfect esteem which your merit and that of Mrs. Bellini have produced, and which will forever enable me to assure you of the sincere regard with which I am Dear Sir Your friend & servant . . .

To Danbury Baptists
January 1, 1802

Jefferson often responded to immediate and contingent situations by articulating what he took to be the universal truth of the subject. Here, in response to a letter of appreciation from the Baptists of Danbury, Connecticut, the third president of the United States coined the phrase "wall of separation between Church & state." Jefferson could not have known at the time that this felicitous phrase would eventually be invoked by the US court system, including the Supreme Court of the United States, as a succinct representation of the intent of the First Amendment of the Constitution. Freedom of conscience was one of the handful of Jefferson's most cherished principles. He was not at all anti-religious, but he did not want the government of the United States to encourage or discourage private religious experience. Recent scholarship has shown that Jefferson originally wrote "wall of eternal separation," but softened the pronouncement a bit before sending the letter on to Connecticut. I have printed here the entire letter, which was addressed to Nehemiah Dodge, Ephraim Robbins, & Stephen S. Nelson, a committee of the Danbury Baptist association in Connecticut.

Gentlemen,

The affectionate sentiments of esteem and approbation which you are so good as to express towards me, on behalf of the Danbury Baptist association, give me the highest satisfaction. my duties dictate a faithful and zealous pursuit of the interests of my constituents, & in proportion as they are persuaded of my fidelity to those duties, the discharge of them becomes more and more pleasing.

Believing with you that religion is a matter which lies solely between Man & his God, that he owes account to none other for his faith or his worship, that the legitimate powers of government reach actions only, & not opinions, I contemplate with sovereign reverence that act of the whole American people which declared that their legislature should "make no law respecting an establishment of religion, or prohibiting the free exercise thereof," thus building a wall of separation between Church & State. Adhering to this expression of the supreme will of the nation in behalf of the rights of conscience, I shall see with sincere satisfaction the progress of those sentiments which tend to restore to man all his natural rights, convinced he has no natural right in opposition to his social duties.

I reciprocate your kind prayers for the protection & blessing of the common father and creator of man, and tender you for yourselves & your religious association, assurances of my high respect & esteem.

To David Rittenhouse
Monticello, July 19, 1778

Who would not have been thrilled to receive this fan letter? Rittenhouse was America's most distinguished mathematician. Jefferson believed Rittenhouse should be exempted from having to earn a living doing tasks that many others could do as well. Today, Jefferson would have recommended Rittenhouse for a MacArthur Prize or an endowed chair at a public university. The "mechanical representation" that Rittenhouse had built was an orrery (a planetarium) designed to display in miniature the workings of the solar system. Jefferson tells Rittenhouse that there is only one better solar system in existence—the one the Creator built! Jefferson wanted a Rittenhouse orrery for his collection of scientific instruments at Monticello. Rittenhouse's orrery can still be viewed at the University of Pennsylvania.

Dear Sir

Writing to a philosopher, I may hope to be pardoned for intruding some thoughts of my own, tho' they relate to him personally. Your time for two years past has, I believe, been principally employed in the civil government of your country. Tho' I have been aware of the authority our cause would acquire with the world from it's being known that yourself and Doctor Franklin were zealous friends to it, and am myself duly impressed with a sense of the arduousness of government, and the obligation those are under who are able to conduct it, yet I am also satisfied there is an order of geniuses above that obligation, and therefore exempted from it. Nobody can conceive that nature ever intended to throw away a Newton upon the occupations of a crown. It would have been a prodigality for which even the conduct of providence might have been arraigned, had he been by birth annexed to what was so far below him. Cooperating with nature in her ordinary economy, we should dispose of and employ the geniuses of men according to their several orders and degrees. I doubt not there are in your country many persons equal to the task of conducting government: but you should consider that the world has but one Rittenhouse, and that it never had one before. The amazing mechanical representation of the solar system which you conceived and executed, has never been surpassed by any but the work of which it is a copy. Are those powers then, which being intended for the erudition of the world, like air and light, the world's common property, to be taken from their proper pursuit to do the commonplace drudgery of governing a single state, a work which may be executed by men of an ordinary stature, such as are always and everywhere to be found? Without having ascended mount Sinai for inspiration, I can pronounce that the precept, in the decalogue of the vulgar, that they shall not make to themselves 'the likeness of anything that is in the heavens above' is reversed for you, and that you will fulfill the highest purposes of your creation by employing yourself in the perpetual breach of that inhibition. For my own country in particular you must remember something like a promise that it should be adorned with one of them. The taking of your city by the enemy has hitherto prevented the proposition from being made and approved by our legislature. The zeal of a true Whig in science must excuse the hazarding these free thoughts, which flow from a desire of promoting the diffusion of knowledge and of your fame, and from one who can assure you truly that he is with much sincerity & esteem Your most obedt. & most humble servant,

To John Breckinridge
Monticello August 12, 1803

This is one of my favorite Jefferson letters. Why? First, he was so committed to strict construction of the US Constitution that he believed it may be necessary to circulate a constitutional amendment to authorize the Louisiana Purchase. Second, it is clear that Jefferson saw the future of American destiny in the West. Free navigation of the Mississippi was a principle he worked hard to secure for the American republic, often in the face of Federalist indifference. Third, I love it that the eternally optimistic and orderly Jefferson could imagine America expanding to the west "range after range, advancing compactly as we multiply." In his plan for the government of the Western Territories of 1784, Jefferson laid out fourteen new square, compact states, gave them names from classical and Native American languages, and assumed that we would fill those two tiers of new states before we added further ranges to the west. Fourth, here Jefferson serenely imagines that the trans-Appalachian territory may wish to establish its own sovereign republic, a sister or cousin to the United States, but not necessarily part of the US.

Dear Sir

The enclosed letter, tho' directed to you, was intended to me also, was left open with a request that, when perused, I would forward it to you. it gives me occasion to write a word to you on the subject of Louisiana, which being a new one, an interchange of sentiment may produce correct ideas before we are to act on them. our information as to the country is very incomplete: we have taken measures to obtain it full as to the settled part which I hope to receive in time for Congress. the boundaries which I deem not admitting question are the high lands on the Western side of the Mississippi enclosing all its waters, the Missouri of course, and terminating in the line drawn from the Northwestern point of the lake of the woods to the nearest source of the Mispi as lately settled between Gr. Britain & us. we have some claims to extend on the seacoast Westwardly to the Rio Norte or Bravo, and better to go Eastwardly to the Rio Perdido, between Mobile & Pensacola, the antient boundary of Louisiana. these claims will be a subject of negotiation with Spain, and if, as soon as she is at war, we push them strongly with one hand, holding out a price in the other, we shall certainly obtain the Floridas, and all in good time. in the meanwhile, without waiting for permission, we shall enter into the exercise of the natural right we have always insisted on with Spain; to wit that of a nation holding the upper part of streams, having a right of innocent passage thro' them to the ocean. we shall prepare her to see us practice on this, & she will not oppose it by force. objections are raising to the Eastward against this vast extent of our boundaries, and propositions are made to exchange Louisiana or a part of it for the Floridas. but, as I have said, we shall get the Floridas without, and I would not give one inch of the waters of the Mississippi to any nation, because I see in a light very important to our peace, the exclusive right to its navigation, & the admission of no nation into it, but as into the Potomak or Delaware, with our consent & under our police. these Federalists see in this acquisition, the formation of a new confederacy embracing all the waters of the Mispi, on both sides of it, and a separation of its Eastern waters from us. these combinations depend on so many circumstances which we cannot foresee, that I place little reliance on them. we have seldom seen neighborhood produce affection among nations. the reverse is almost the universal truth. besides if it should become the great interest of those nations to separate from this, if their happiness should depend on it so strongly as to induce them to go through that convulsion, why should the Atlantic states dread it? but especially why should we, their present inhabitants, take side in such a question? when I view the Atlantic states, procuring for those on the Eastern waters of the Mispi, friendly instead of hostile neighbors on its western waters, I do not view it as an Englishman would the procuring future blessings for the French nation with whom he has no relations of blood or affection. the future inhabitants of the Atlantic & Mississippi states will be our sons. we leave them in distinct but bordering establishments. we think we see their happiness in their union, & we wish it. events may prove it otherwise; and if they see their interest in separation, why should we take side with our Atlantic rather than our Mispi descendants? it is the elder & the younger son differing. god bless them both, & keep them in union if it be for their good, but separate them if it be better. the inhabited part of Louisiana, from Point coupeé to the sea will of course be immediately a territorial government & soon a state. but above that, the best use we can make of the country for some time will be to give establishments in it to the Indians on the East side of the Mispi in exchange for their present country, and open land offices in the last, & thus make this acquisition the means of filling up the Eastern side instead of drawing off it's population. when we shall be full on this side, we may lay off a range of states on the Western bank from the head to the mouth, & so range after range, advancing compactly as we multiply. This treaty must of course be laid before both houses, because both have important functions to exercise respecting it. they I presume will see their duty to their country in ratifying & paying for it, so as to secure a good which would otherwise probably be never again in their power. but I suppose they must then appeal to the nation for an additional article to the constitution, approving & confirming an act which the nation had not previously authorized. the constitution has made no provision for our holding foreign territory, still less for incorporating foreign nations into our union. the Executive in seizing the fugitive occurrence which so much advanced the good of their country, have done an act beyond the constitution. the legislature in casting behind them Metaphysical subtleties, and risking themselves like faithful servants, must ratify & pay for it, and throw themselves on their country for doing for them unauthorized what we know they would have done for themselves had they been in a situation to do it. it is the case of a guardian, investing the money of his ward in purchasing an important adjacent territory; & saying to him when of age, I did this for your good; I pretend to no right to bind you. you may disavow me, and I must get out of the scrape as I can. I thought it my duty to risk myself for you. but we shall not be disavowed by the nation, and their act of indemnity will confirm & not weaken the constitution, by more strongly marking out its lines.

To John Adams
Monticello, October 28, 1813

This is one of the most important letters Jefferson ever wrote. Once Benjamin Rush managed to bring the two great patriarchs back into correspondence—and eventually friendship—they attempted very carefully to air their differences and to try to find common ground. Adams worked harder at this than Jefferson, a harmony obsessive who had no interest in disputing anything with his crabby old friend. Still, they tried, as Adams suggested, to explain themselves to each other. Their fourteen-year correspondence is one of the greatest treasures of American history. At this point—fairly early on in the retirement correspondence—Jefferson and Adams tried to decide what kind of aristocracy America could endure, if any. Adams' view was that class hierarchy and maldistribution of the fruits of life are inevitable, and that no amount of social engineering would ever eliminate special privilege. In fact, said Adams, we may as well give the aristocrats the Senate, where we can keep an eye on them. Jefferson countered with this masterpiece of American idealism: that here, in America, as in all true republics, we should seek out natural aristocrats, born in every stratum of life, and lift them to positions of leadership in culture and in public life; and at the same time a true republic should do what it can to discourage pseudo-aristocracy, the domination of artificially-derived privilege over merit. One of the things I most love about Thomas Jefferson is that while he was born with a silver spoon in his mouth, he gave his life to the creation of a society more equal and egalitarian (slavery excepted) than any civilization in history.

Dear Sir,

[For] I agree with you that there is a natural aristocracy among men. the grounds of this are virtue & talents. formerly bodily powers gave place among the aristoi. but since the invention of gunpowder has armed the weak as well as the strong with missile death, bodily strength, like beauty, good humor, politeness and other accomplishments, has become but an auxiliary ground of distinction. there is also an artificial aristocracy founded on wealth and birth, without either virtue or talents; for with these it would belong to the first class. the natural aristocracy I consider as the most precious gift of nature, for the instruction, the trusts, and government of society and indeed it would have been inconsistent in creation to have formed man for the social state, and not to have provided virtue and wisdom enough to manage the concerns of the society. may we not even say that that form of government is the best which provides the most effectually for a pure selection of these natural aristoi into the offices of government? the artificial aristocracy is a mischievous ingredient in government, and provision should be made to prevent it's ascendancy. on the question, What is the best provision? you and I differ; but we differ as rational friends, using the free exercise of our own reason, and mutually indulging it's errors. you think it best to put the Pseudo-aristoi into a separate chamber of legislation where they may be hindered from doing mischief by their coordinate branches, and where also they may be a protection to wealth against the Agrarian and plundering enterprises of the Majority of the people. I think that to give them power in order to prevent them from doing mischief, is arming them for it, and increasing instead of remedying the evil. for if the coordinate branches can arrest their action, so may they that of the coordinates. mischief may be done negatively as well as positively. of this a cabal in the Senate of the US. has furnished many proofs. nor do I believe them necessary to protect the wealthy; because enough of these will find their way into every branch of the legislature to protect themselves. from 15 to 20 legislatures of our own, in action for 30 years past, have proved that no fears of an equalization of property are to be apprehended from them. I think the best remedy is exactly that provided by all our constitutions, to leave to the citizens the free election and separation of the aristoi from the pseudo-aristoi, of the wheat from the chaff. in general they will elect the real good and wise. in some instances, wealth may corrupt, and birth blind them; but not in sufficient degree to endanger the society.

It is probable that our difference of opinion may in some measure be produced by a difference of character in those among whom we live. from what I have seen of Massachusetts and Connecticut myself, and still more from what I have heard, and the character given of the former by yourself, who know them so much better, there seems to be in those two states a traditionary reverence for certain families, which has rendered the offices of the government nearly hereditary in those families. I presume that from an early period of your history, members of these families happening to possess virtue and talents, have honestly exercised them for the good of the people, and by their services have endeared their names to them. in coupling Connecticut with you, I mean it politically only, not morally. for having made the Bible the Common law of their land they seem to have modelled their morality on the story of Jacob and Laban. but altho' this hereditary succession to office with you may in some degree be founded in real family merit, yet in a much higher degree it has proceeded from your strict alliance of church and state. these families are canonized in the eyes of the people on the common principle 'you tickle me, and I will tickle you.' in Virginia we have nothing of this. our clergy, before the revolution, having been secured against rivalship by fixed salaries, did not give themselves the trouble of acquiring influence over the people. of wealth, there were great accumulations in particular families, handed down from generation to generation under the English law of entails. but the only object of ambition for the wealthy was a seat in the king's council. all their court then was paid to the crown and it's creatures; and they Philipised in all collisions between the king & people, hence they were unpopular; and that unpopularity continues attached to their names. a Randolph, a Carter, or a Burwell must have great personal superiority over a common competitor to be elected by the people, even at this day. at the first session of our legislature after the Declaration of Independence, we passed a law abolishing entails. and this was followed by one abolishing the privilege of Primogeniture, and dividing the lands of intestates equally among all their children, or other representatives. these laws, drawn by myself, laid the axe to the root of Pseudo-aristocracy. and had another which I prepared been adopted by the legislature, our work would have been complete. it was a Bill for the more general diffusion of learning. this proposed to divide every county into wards of 5 or 6 miles square, like your townships; to establish in each ward a free school for reading, writing and common arithmetic; to provide for the annual selection of the best subjects from these schools who might receive at the public expense a higher degree of education at a district school; and from these district schools to select a certain number of the most promising subjects to be completed at

an University, where all the useful sciences should be taught.
worth and genius would thus have been sought out from
every condition of life, and completely prepared by education
for defeating the competition of wealth & birth for public
trusts. my proposition had for a further object to impart
to these wards those portions of self-government for which
they are best qualified, by confiding to them the care of their
poor, their roads, police, elections, the nomination of jurors,
administration of justice in small cases, elementary exercises
of militia, in short, to have made them little republics, with
a Warden at the head of each, for all those concerns which,
being under their eye, they would better manage than the
larger republics of the county or state. a general call of ward-
meetings by their Wardens on the same day thro' the state
would at any time produce the genuine sense of the people on
any required point, and would enable the state to act in mass,
as your people have so often done, and with so much effect,
by their town-meetings. the law for religious freedom, which
made a part of this system, having put down the aristocracy
of the clergy, and restored to the citizen the freedom of the
mind, and those of entails and descents nurturing an equality
of condition among them, this on Education would have
raised the mass of the people to the high ground of moral
respectability necessary to their own safety, & to orderly
government; and would have completed the great object of
qualifying them to select the veritable aristoi, for the trusts
of government, to the exclusion of the Pseudalists. . . .

With respect to Aristocracy we should further consider that,
before the establishment of the American states, nothing
was known to History but the Man of the old world, crowded
within limits either small or overcharged, and steeped in the
vices which that situation generates. a government adapted

to such men would be one thing; but a very different one that for the Man of these states. here everyone may have land to labor for himself if he chooses; or, preferring the exercise of any other industry, may exact for it such compensation as not only to afford a comfortable subsistence, but wherewith to provide for a cessation from labor in old age. everyone, by his property, or by his satisfactory situation, is interested in the support of law and order. and such men may safely and advantageously reserve to themselves a wholesome control over their public affairs, and a degree of freedom, which in the hands of the Canaille of the cities of Europe, would be instantly perverted to the demolition and destruction of everything public and private. the history of the last 25. years of France, and of the last 40 years in America, nay of its last 200 years, proves the truth of both parts of this observation.

But even in Europe a change has sensibly taken place in the mind of Man. science had liberated the ideas of those who read and reflect, and the American example had kindled feelings of right in the people. an insurrection has consequently begun, of science, talents & courage against rank and birth, which have fallen into contempt. it has failed in its first effort, because the mobs of the cities, the instrument used for its accomplishment, debased by ignorance, poverty and vice, could not be restrained to rational action. but the world will recover from the panic of this first catastrophe. science is progressive, and talents and enterprise on the alert. resort may be had to the people of the country, a more governable power from their principles & subordination; and rank and birth and tinsel-aristocracy will finally shrink into insignificance even there. this however we have no right to meddle with. it suffices for us, if the moral & physical condition of our own citizens qualifies them to select the able and good for the direction of their government, with a recurrence of elections at such short periods as will enable them to displace an unfaithful servant before the mischief he meditates may be irremediable.

I have thus stated my opinion on a point on which we differ, not with a view to controversy, for we are both too old to change opinions which are the result of a long life of enquiry and reflection; but on the suggestion of a former letter of yours that we ought not to die before we have explained ourselves to each other. we acted in perfect harmony thro' a long and perilous contest for our liberty and independence. a constitution has been acquired which, tho neither of us think perfect, yet both consider as competent to render our fellow citizens the happiest and the securest on whom the sun has ever shone. if we do not think exactly alike as to its imperfections, it matters little to our country which, after devoting to it long lives of disinterested labor, we have delivered over to our successors in life, who will be able to take care of it, and of themselves.

To James Monroe
Monticello, May 20, 1782

Jefferson was not a particularly good governor of Virginia (1779–81). The war for American independence came home to Virginia during his time in office. He attended to the enormous press of emergency business with his usual administrative mastery, but he was decidedly civilian in his approach, and no part of him was willing to take on quasi-dictatorial powers even to save Virginia in its hour of need. When Banastre Tarleton raided Monticello with his dragoons on June 4, 1781, Jefferson and his family slipped away to safety on a nearby mountain. The better part of valor may have been to live to fight another day, but some people in Virginia, including Patrick Henry, accused Jefferson of cowardice. The war soon ended at Yorktown and Jefferson was handsomely exonerated by the Virginia House of Delegates, but he never got over the humiliation. It made him a better president (1801–09), because he seems to have determined never again to interpret his official powers in a narrow and cautious way. I find Jefferson's declaration that prolonged government service would be "slavery and not that liberty which the bill of rights has made inviolable" disturbing, because it cheapens the word slavery and inadvertently exposes Jefferson to the charges of insensitivity and hypocrisy. It is also interesting to note that in 1803 President Jefferson seems to have forgotten this passionate declaration of independence when he pressured the very same James Monroe to undertake an important diplomatic mission for the United States.

Dear Sir

I have been gratified with the receipt of your two favors of the 6th. and 11th. inst. It gives me pleasure that your county has been wise enough to enlist your talents into their service. I am much obliged by the kind wishes you express of seeing me also in Richmond and am always mortified when anything is expected from me which I cannot fulfill, and more especially if it relate to the public service. Before I ventured to declare to my countrymen my determination to retire from public employment I examined well my heart to know whether it were thoroughly cured of every principle of political ambition, whether no lurking particle remained which might leave me uneasy when reduced within the limits of mere private life. I became satisfied that every fiber of that passion was thoroughly eradicated. I examined also in other views my right to withdraw. I considered that I had been thirteen years engaged in public service, that during that time I had so totally abandoned all attention to my private affairs as to permit them to run into great disorder and ruin, that I had now a family advanced to years which require my attention and instruction, that to this was added the hopeful offspring of a deceased friend whose memory must be forever dear to me who have no other reliance for being rendered useful to themselves and their country, that by a constant sacrifice of time, labor, loss, parental and friendly duties, I had been so far from gaining the affection of my countrymen which was the only reward I ever asked or could have felt, that I had even lost the small estimation I before possessed: that however I might have comforted myself under the disapprobation of the well-meaning but uninformed people yet that of their representatives was a shock on which I had not calculated: that this indeed had been followed by an exculpatory declaration, but in the mean time I had been suspected and suspended in the eyes of the world without the least hint then or afterwards made public which might restrain them from supposing I stood arraigned for treasons of the heart and not mere weaknesses of the head. And I felt that these injuries, for such they have been since acknowledged, had inflicted a wound on my spirit which will only be cured by the all-healing grave. If reason and inclination unite in justifying my retirement, the laws of my country are equally in favor of it. Whether the state may command the political services of all it's members to an indefinite extent, or if these be among the rights never wholly ceded to the public power, is a question which I do not find expressly decided in England. Obiter dictums on the subject I have indeed met with, but the completion of the times in which these have dropped would generally answer them, and besides that, this species of authority is not acknowledged in our profession. In this country however since the present government has been established the point has been settled by uniform, pointed, and multiplied precedents. Offices of every kind, and given by every power, have been daily and hourly declined and resigned from the declaration of independence to this moment. The General assembly has accepted these without discrimination of office, and without ever questioning them in point of right. If a difference between the office of a delegate and any other could ever have been supposed, yet in the case of Mr. Thompson Mason who declined the office of delegate and was permitted by the house so to do that supposition has been proved to be groundless. But indeed no such distinction of offices can be admitted; reason and the opinions of the lawyers putting all on a footing as to this question and giving to the delegate the aid of all the precedents of the refusal of other offices, the law then does not warrant the assumption of such a power by the state over it's members. For if it does where is that law? Nor yet does reason, for tho' I will admit that this does subject every individual if called on to an equal tour of political duty, yet it can never go so far as to submit to it his whole existence. If we are made in some degree for others, yet in a greater are we made for ourselves. It were contrary to feeling and indeed ridiculous to suppose a man had less right in himself than one of his neighbors or all of them put together. This would be slavery and not that liberty which the bill of rights has made inviolable and for the preservation of which our government has been changed. Nothing could so completely divest us of that liberty as the establishment of the opinion that the state has a perpetual right to the services of all it's members. This to men of certain ways of thinking would be to annihilate the blessing of existence; to contradict the giver of life who gave it for happiness and not for wretchedness, and certainly to such it were better that they had never been born. However with these I may think public service and private misery inseparably linked together, I have not the vanity to count myself among those whom the state would think worth oppressing with perpetual service. I have received a sufficient memento to the contrary. I am persuaded that having hitherto dedicated to them the whole of the active and useful part of my life I shall be permitted to pass the rest in mental quiet. I hope too that I did not mistake the mode any more than the matter of right when I preferred a simple act of renunciation to the taking sanctuary under those many disqualifications (provided by the law for other purposes indeed but) which afford asylum also for rest to the wearied. I dare say you did not expect by the few words you dropped on the right of renunciation to expose yourself to the fatigue of so long a letter, but I wished you to see that if I had done wrong I had been betrayed by a semblance of right at least.

To Dr. Edward Jenner
May 14, 1806

Again, who would not have been honored to receive this fan letter from the sitting president of the United States? Edward Jenner had discovered the true smallpox vaccine, a dramatic improvement over the previous inoculation method that worked (sometimes) by giving the patient a small dose of smallpox and hoping she or he had a strong enough immune system to survive it. Jenner noticed English milkmaids routinely got kinepox from cattle, a cousin to smallpox that was not life-threatening and not disfiguring. This gave them lifelong immunity to smallpox. When Jefferson learned of this profound medical breakthrough, he picked up his pen and wrote this famous letter, which he did not share with the media! In other words, he wrote the letter as a pure tribute, not to call attention to himself as a man of enlightenment. Today's perplexing debate about vaccination would benefit from a brief study of smallpox. Medical historians have estimated that at least two billion people worldwide died of smallpox before vaccination got the best of it. Now one of the most dreaded diseases in human history has been reduced to one strain in one petri dish.

Sir,

I have received a copy of the evidence at large respecting the discovery of the vaccine inoculation which you have been pleased to send me, and for which I return you my thanks. Having been among the early converts, in this part of the globe, to its efficiency, I took an early part in recommending it to my countrymen. I avail myself of this occasion of rendering you a portion of the tribute of gratitude due to you from the whole human family. Medicine has never before produced any single improvement of such utility. Harvey's discovery of the circulation of the blood was a beautiful addition to our knowledge of the animal economy, but on a review of the practice of medicine before and since that epoch, I do not see any great amelioration which has been derived from that discovery. You have erased from the calendar of human afflictions one of its greatest. Yours is the comfortable reflection that mankind can never forget that you have lived. Future nations will know by history only that the loathsome small pox has existed and by you has been extirpated.

Accept my fervent wishes for your health and happiness and assurances of the greatest respect and consideration.

To Elbridge Gerry
Philadelphia, January 26, 1799

Nowadays we have two long-established political parties, and they have developed nearly identical electoral protocols. That was not true in Jefferson's time, when the two-party system was just beginning to emerge. When Jefferson stood (reluctantly) for the presidency in 1800 he made no public appearances. There were the beginnings of caucuses, but no conventions, no primaries, no party platforms. Still, Jefferson wanted to make his views known to the American people, and he used this letter to his friend Elbridge Gerry to outline his core political principles. He knew that Gerry would take extracts from the letter (much longer than the passage reprinted here) and share them with his network of friends, and they in turn would copy what they read and pass on Jefferson's "platform" to others. It sounds like an inefficient way to get the word out, but it was all the social network Jefferson had. The letter is a magnificent exposition of Jefferson's outlook and his vision of America.

My Dear Sir,

I do then with sincere zeal wish an inviolable preservation of our present federal constitution, according to the true sense in which it was adopted by the states, that in which it was advocated by it's friends, & not that which it's enemies apprehended, who therefore became its enemies: and I am opposed to the monarchizing it's features by the forms of its administration, with a view to conciliate a first transition to a President & Senate for life, & from that to a hereditary tenure of these offices, & thus to worm out the elective principle. I am for preserving to the states the powers not yielded by them to the Union, & to the legislature of the Union it's constitutional share in the division of powers: and I am not for transferring all the powers of the states to the general government, & all those of that government to the Executive branch. I am for a government rigorously frugal & simple, applying all the possible savings of the public revenue to the discharge of the national debt: and not for a multiplication of officers & salaries merely to make partisans, & for increasing, by every device, the public debt, on the principle of it's being a public blessing. I am for relying, for internal defense, on our militia solely till actual invasion, and for such a naval force only as may protect our coasts and harbors from such depredations as we have experienced: and not for a standing army in time of peace which may overawe the public sentiment; nor for a navy which by its own expenses and the eternal wars in which it will implicate us, will grind us with public burthens, & sink us under them. I am for free commerce with all nations, political connection with none, & little or no diplomatic establishment: and I am not for linking ourselves, by new treaties with the quarrels of Europe, entering that field of slaughter to preserve their balance, or joining in the confederacy of kings to war against the principles of liberty. I am for freedom of religion, & against all maneuvers to bring about a legal ascendancy of one sect over another: for freedom of the press, & against all violations of the constitution to silence by force & not by reason the complaints or criticisms, just or unjust, of our citizens against the conduct of their agents. and I am for encouraging the progress of science in all it's branches; and not for raising a hue and cry against the sacred name of philosophy, for awing the human mind, by stories of raw head & bloody bones, to a distrust of its own vision & to repose implicitly on that of others; to go backwards instead of forwards to look for improvement, to believe that government, religion, morality & every other science were in the highest perfection in ages of the darkest ignorance, and that nothing can ever be devised more perfect than what was established by our forefathers. to these I will add that I was a sincere well-wisher to the success of the French revolution, and still wish it may end in the establishment of a free & well-ordered republic: but I have not been insensible under the atrocious depredations they have committed on our commerce. the first object of my heart is my own country. in that is embarked my family, my fortune, & my own existence. I have not one farthing of interest, nor one fiber of attachment out of it, nor a single motive of preference of any one nation to another but in proportion as they are more or less friendly to us. but though deeply feeling the injuries of France, I did not think war the surest mode of redressing them. I did believe that a mission sincerely disposed to preserve peace, would obtain for us a peaceable & honorable settlement and retribution; & I appeal to you to say whether this might not have been obtained, if either of your colleagues had been of the same sentiment with yourself.—these my friend are my principles; they are unquestionably the principles of the great body of our fellow citizens, and I know there is not one of them which is not yours also. in truth we never differed but on one ground, the funding system; and as from the moment of it's being adopted by the constituted authorities, I became religiously principled in the sacred discharge of it to the uttermost farthing, we are now united even on that single ground of difference.

You suppose that you have been abused by both parties. as far as has come to my knowledge you are misinformed. I have never seen or heard a sentence of blame uttered against you by the republicans, unless we were so to construe their wishes that you had more boldly cooperated in a project of a treaty, and would more explicitly state whether there was in your colleagues that flexibility which persons earnest after peace would have practiced? whether, on the contrary, their demeanor was not cold, reserved and distant at least, if not backward? and whether, if they had yielded to those informal conferences which Taleyrand seems to have courted, the liberal accommodation you suppose might not have been effected, even with their agency? your fellow citizens think they have a right to full information in a case of such great concernment to them. it is their sweat which is to earn all the expenses of the war, and their blood which is to flow in expiation of the causes of it. it may be in your power to save them from these miseries by full communications and unrestrained details, postponing motives of delicacy to those of duty. it rests with you to come forward independently, to take your stand on the high ground of your own character, to disregard calumny, and to be borne above it on the shoulders of your grateful fellow citizens, or to sink into the humble oblivion to which the Federalists (self-called) have secretly condemned you, and even to be happy if they will indulge you with oblivion while they have beamed on your colleagues meridian splendor. pardon me, my dear Sir, if my expressions are strong. my feelings are so much more so, that it is with difficulty I reduce them even to the tone I use. if you doubt the dispositions towards you, look into the papers on both sides for the toasts which were given through all the states on the 4th. of July. you will there see whose hearts were with you, and whose were ulcerated against you. indeed as soon as it was known that you had consented to stay in Paris, there was no measure observed in the execrations of the war-party. they openly wished you might be guillotined, or sent to Cayenne, or anything else: and these expressions were finally stifled from a principle of policy only, & to prevent you from being urged to a justification of yourself. from this principle alone proceeds the silence, & cold respect they observe towards you. still they cannot prevent at times the flames bursting from under the embers, as mr Pickering's letters, report, & conversations testify as well as the indecent expressions respecting you indulged by some of them in the debate on these dispatches. these sufficiently shew that you are never more to be honored or trusted by them, & that they wait to crush you forever only till they can do it without danger to themselves.

To Thomas Jefferson Randolph
Washington, November 24, 1808

This is one of Jefferson's greatest letters. His grandson Thomas Jefferson Randolph (Jeff) was leaving the safe environs of Virginia to pursue education in New England. His grandfather knew that Jeff would soon be surrounded by anti-Jeffersonians, Federalists, and Calvinists and that he would be subjected to proxy criticism and almost certainly drawn into disputation. It is in this letter that Jefferson articulates his concept of "artificial good humor," by which he means exhibiting concerted civility even under stressful circumstances. Clearly Jefferson learned more from Benjamin Franklin than a tedious story about the design of a hat sign in Philadelphia! In this letter Jefferson has a rare moment of humor when he writes, "When I hear another express an opinion, which is not mine, I say to myself, He has a right to his opinion, as I to mine; why should I question it. His error does me no injury." When Jefferson wrote this beautiful letter he was probably remembering that Alexander Hamilton's son Philip was cut down in a duel, defending his father's honor, on November 23, 1801. Thomas Jefferson Randolph survived his sojourn in Federalist territory and went on to be his grandfather's greatest support in the retirement years.

My Dear Jefferson,

I have just received the enclosed letter under cover from Mr. Bankhead which I presume is from Anne and will inform you she is well. Mr. Bankhead has consented to go and pursue his studies at Monticello, and live with us till his pursuits or circumstances may require a separate establishment. Your situation, thrown at such a distance from us and alone, cannot but give us all, great anxieties for you. As much has been secured for you, by your particular position and the acquaintance to which you have been recommended, as could be done towards shielding you from the dangers which surround you. But thrown on a wide world, among entire strangers without a friend or guardian to advise so young too and with so little experience of mankind, your dangers are great, and still your safety must rest on yourself. A determination never to do what is wrong, prudence, and good humor, will go far towards securing to you the estimation of the world. When I recollect that at 14. years of age, the whole care and direction of my self was thrown on myself entirely, without a relation or friend qualified to advise or guide me, and recollect the various sorts of bad company with which I associated from time to time, I am astonished I did not turn off with some of them, and become as worthless to society as they were. I had the good fortune to become acquainted very early with some characters of very high standing, and to feel the incessant wish that I could even become what they were. Under temptations and difficulties, I could ask myself what would Dr. Small, Mr. Wythe, Peyton Randolph do in this situation? What course in it will ensure me their approbation? I am certain that this mode of deciding on my conduct tended more to its correctness than any reasoning powers I possessed. Knowing the even and dignified line they pursued, I could never doubt for a moment which of two courses would be in character for them. Whereas seeking the same object through a process of moral reasoning, and with the jaundiced eye of youth, I should often have erred. From the circumstances of my position I was often thrown into the society of horse racers, cardplayers, Foxhunters, scientific and professional men, and of dignified men; and many a time have I asked myself, in the enthusiastic moment of the death of a fox, the victory of a favorite horse, the issue of a question eloquently argued at the bar or in the great Council of the nation, well, which of these kinds of reputation should I prefer? That of a horse jockey? A foxhunter? An Orator? Or the honest advocate of my country's rights? Be assured my dear Jefferson, that these little returns into ourselves, this self-catechizing habit, is not trifling, nor useless, but leads to the prudent selection and steady pursuits of what is right. I have mentioned good humor as one of the preservatives of our peace and tranquility. It is among the most effectual, and it's effect is so well imitated and aided artificially by politeness, that this also becomes an acquisition of first rate value. In truth, politeness is artificial good humor, it covers the natural want of it, and ends by rendering habitual a substitute nearly equivalent to the real virtue. It is the practice of sacrificing to those whom we meet in society all the little conveniences and preferences which will gratify them, and deprive us of nothing worth a moment's consideration; it is the giving a pleasing and flattering turn to our expressions which will conciliate others, and make them pleased with us as well as themselves. How cheap a price for the good will of another! When this is in return for a rude thing said by another, it brings him to his senses, it mortifies and corrects him in the most salutary way, and places him at the feet of your good nature in the eyes of the company. But in stating prudential rules for our government in society I must not omit the important one of never entering into dispute or argument with another. I never yet saw an instance of one of two disputants convincing the other by argument. I have seen many on their getting warm, becoming rude, and shooting one another. Conviction is the effect of our own dispassionate reasoning, either in solitude, or weighing within ourselves dispassionately what we hear from others standing uncommitted in argument ourselves. It was one of the rules which above all others made Doctor Franklin the most amiable of men in society, 'never to contradict anybody.' If he was urged to announce an opinion, he did it rather by asking questions, as if for information, or by suggesting doubts. When I hear another express an opinion, which is not mine, I say to myself, He has a right to his opinion, as I to mine; why should I question it. His error does me no injury, and shall I become a Don Quixot to bring all men by force of argument, to one opinion? If a fact be misstated, it is probable he is gratified by a belief of it, and I have no right to deprive him of the gratification. If he wants information he will ask it, and then I will give it in measured terms; but if he still believes his own story, and shows a desire to dispute the fact with me, I hear him and say nothing. It is his affair, not mine, if he prefers error. There are two classes of disputants most frequently to be met with among us. The first is of young students just entered the threshold of science, with a first view of its outlines, not yet filled up with the details and modifications which a further progress would bring to their knowledge. The other consists of the ill-tempered and rude men in society who have taken up a passion for politics. (Good humor and politeness never introduce into mixed society a question on which they foresee there will be a difference of opinion.) From both of these classes of disputants, my dear Jefferson, keep aloof, as you would from the infected subjects of yellow fever or pestilence. Consider yourself, when with them, as among the patients of Bedlam needing medical more than moral counsel. Be a listener only, keep within yourself, and endeavor to establish with yourself the habit of silence, especially in politics. In the fevered state of our country, no good can ever result from any attempt to set one of these fiery zealots to rights either in fact or principle. They are determined as to the facts they will believe, and the opinions on which they will act. Get by them, therefore as you would by an angry bull: it is not for a man of sense to dispute the road with such an animal. You will be more exposed than others to have these animals shaking their horns at you, because of the relation in which you stand with me and to hate me as a chief in the antagonist party your presence will be to them what the vomit-grass is to the sick dog a nostrum for producing an ejaculation. Look upon them exactly with that eye, and pity them as objects to whom you can administer only occasional ease. My character is not within their power. It is in the hands of my fellow citizens at large, and will be consigned to honor or infamy by the verdict of the republican mass of our country, according to what themselves will have seen, not what their enemies and mine shall have said. Never therefore consider these puppies in politics as requiring any notice from you, and always shew that you are not afraid to leave my character to the umpirage of public opinion. Look steadily to the pursuits which have carried you to Philadelphia, be very select in the society you attach yourself to; avoid taverns, drinkers, smoakers, and idlers and dissipated persons generally; for it is with such that broils and contentions arise, and you will find your path more easy and tranquil.

The limits of my paper warn me that it is time for me to close with my affectionate Adieux.

P. S. Present me affectionately to Mr. Ogilvie, and in doing the same to Mr. Peale tell him I am writing with his polygraph and shall send him mine the first moment I have leisure enough to pack it.

To James Madison
Paris, September 6, 1789

I print this letter in its entirety because it is one of Jefferson's most important letters. Everyone interested in the principles of representation and consent of the governed should study this letter. During this fertile period in Jefferson's life, as he watched France descend into revolution and, eventually, a reign of terror, Jefferson tried to determine what had gone wrong in France and how the United States could avoid making similar mistakes. Jefferson often—and especially during this period—sent trial balloons to James Madison's Montpelier in Virginia, asking his closest political associate to help him think things through. The ruinous French national debt had brought on the crisis that led to the French Revolution. Jefferson wondered how the United States could avoid passing one generation's fiscal irresponsibility onto the next (and the next) generation. That led to this famous letter, "the earth belongs to the living." Poor Madison was not convinced by his friend's argument (or its logic), but he understood that Jefferson was attempting to make sure things did not get so bankrupt and rootbound in America that a savage American Revolution, like its French counterpart, would become necessary. Jefferson believed that by tearing up the Constitution once every generation (here calculated as about nineteen years) we could avoid chaining ourselves to the dead hand of the past. Madison's response[20] to this letter is a counter-masterpiece. His challenge was to acknowledge Jefferson's genius and his insight, but to take Jefferson's argument apart point by point without offending him and without pretending he did not see the fundamental justice of Jefferson's principle.

---

20   Madison to Thomas Jefferson, Feb 4, 1790

Dear Sir

I sit down to write to you without knowing by what occasion I shall send my letter. I do it because a subject comes into my head which I would wish to develop a little more than is practicable in the hurry of the moment of making up general dispatches.

The question Whether one generation of men has a right to bind another, seems never to have been started either on this or our side of the water. Yet it is a question of such consequences as not only to merit decision, but place also, among the fundamental principles of every government. The course of reflection in which we are immersed here on the elementary principles of society has presented this question to my mind; & that no such obligation can be so transmitted I think very capable of proof. I set out on this ground, which I suppose to be self-evident, 'that the earth belongs in usufruct to the living': that the dead have neither powers nor rights over it. The portion occupied by any individual ceases to be his when himself ceases to be, & reverts to the society. If the society has formed no rules for the appropriation of it's lands in severalty, it will be taken by the first occupants. These will generally be the wife & children of the decedent. If they have formed rules of appropriation, those rules may give it to the wife and children, or to some one of them, or to the legatee of the deceased. So they may give it to his creditor. But the child, the legatee, or creditor takes it, not by any natural right, but by a law of the society of which they are members, & to which they are subject. Then no man can, by natural right, oblige the lands he occupied, or the persons who succeed him in that occupation, to the payment of debts contracted by him. For if he could, he might, during his own life, eat up the usufruct of the lands for several generations to come, & then the lands would belong to the dead, & not to the living, which would be the reverse of our principle.

What is true of every member of the society individually, is true of them all collectively, since the rights of the whole can be no more than the sum of the rights of the individuals. To keep our ideas clear when applying them to a multitude, let us suppose a whole generation of men to be born on the same day, to attain mature age on the same day, & to die on the same day, leaving a succeeding generation in the moment of attaining their mature age all together. Let the ripe age be supposed of 21. years, & their period of life 34. years more, that being the average term given by the bills of mortality to persons who have already attained 21. years of age. Each successive generation would, in this way, come on, and go off the stage at a fixed moment, as individuals do now. Then I say the earth belongs to each of these generations, during it's course, fully, and in their own right. The 2d. generation receives it clear of the debts & incumbrances of the 1st. the 3d of the 2d. & so on. For if the 1st. could charge it with a debt, then the earth would belong to the dead & not the living generation. Then no generation can contract debts greater than may be paid during the course of its own existence. At 21. years of age they may bind themselves & their lands for 34. years to come at 22. for 33: at 23. for 32. and at 54. for one year only; because these are the terms of life which remain to them at those respective epochs. But a material difference must be noted between the succession of an individual, & that of a whole generation. Individuals are parts only of a society, subject to the laws of the whole. These laws may appropriate the portion of land occupied by a decedent to his creditor rather than to any other, or to his child on condition he satisfies the creditor. But when a whole generation, that is, the whole society dies, as in the case we have supposed, and another generation or society succeeds, this forms a whole, and there is no superior who can give their territory to a third society, who may have lent money to their predecessors beyond their faculties of paying.

What is true of a generation all arriving to self-government on the same day, & dying all on the same day, is true of those in a constant course of decay & renewal, with this only difference. A generation coming in & going out entire, as in the first case, would have a right in the 1st. year of their self-dominion to contract a debt for 33. years, in the 10th. for 24. in the 20th. for 14. in the 30th. for 4. whereas generations, changing daily by daily deaths & births, have one constant term, beginning at the date of their contract, and ending when a majority of those of full age at that date shall be dead. The length of that term may be estimated from the tables of mortality, corrected by the circumstances of climate, occupation &c. peculiar to the country of the contractors. Take, for instance, the table of M. de Buffon wherein he states 23,994 deaths, & the ages at which they happened. Suppose a society in which 23,994 persons are born every year, & live to the ages stated in this table. The conditions of that society will be as follows. 1st. It will consist constantly of 617,703. persons of all ages. 2ly. Of those living at any one instant of time, one half will be dead in 24. years 8. months. 3dly. 10,675 will arrive every year at the age of 21. years complete. 4ly. It will constantly have 348,417 persons of all ages above 21. years. 5ly. And the half of those of 21. years & upwards living at any one instant of time will be dead in 18. years 8. months, or say 19. years as the nearest integral number. Then 19. years is the term beyond which neither the representatives of a nation, nor even the whole nation itself assembled, can validly extend a debt.

To render this conclusion palpable by example, suppose that Louis XIV. and XV. had contracted debts in the name of the French nation to the amount of 10,000 milliards of livres, & that the whole had been contracted in Genoa. The interest of this sum would be 500. milliards, which is said to be the whole rent roll or net proceeds of the territory of France. Must the present generation of men have retired from the territory in which nature produced them, & ceded it to the Genoese creditors? No. They have the same rights over the soil on which they were produced, as the preceding generations had. They derive these rights not from their predecessors, but from nature. They then and their soil are by nature clear of the debts of their predecessors.

Again suppose Louis XV. & his cotemporary generation had said to the money-lenders of Genoa, give us money that we may eat, drink, & be merry in our day; and on condition you will demand no interest till the end of 19. years you shall then forever after receive an annual interest of 12⅝ per cent. The money is lent on these conditions, is divided among the living, eaten, drank, & squandered. Would the present generation be obliged to apply the produce of the earth & of their labor to replace their dissipations? Not at all.

I suppose that the received opinion, that the public debts of one generation devolve on the next, has been suggested by our seeing habitually in private life that he who succeeds to lands is required to pay the debts of his ancestor or testator: without considering that this requisition is municipal only, not moral; flowing from the will of the society, which has found it convenient to appropriate lands, become vacant by the death of their occupant, on the condition of a payment of his debts: but that between society & society, or generation

& generation, there is no municipal obligation, no umpire but the law of nature. We seem not to have perceived that, by the law of nature, one generation is to another as one independent nation to another.

The interest of the national debt of France being in fact but a two thousandth part of it's rent roll, the payment of it is practicable enough: & so becomes a question merely of honor, or of expediency. But with respect to future debts, would it not be wise & just for that nation to declare, in the constitution they are forming, that neither the legislature, nor the nation itself, can validly contract more debt than they may pay within their own age, or within the term of 19. years? and that all future contracts will be deemed void as to what shall remain unpaid at the end of 19. years from their date? This would put the lenders, & the borrowers also, on their guard. By reducing too the faculty of borrowing within its natural limits, it would bridle the spirit of war, to which too free a course has been procured by the inattention of money-lenders to this law of nature, that succeeding generations are not responsible for the preceding.

On similar ground it may be proved that no society can make a perpetual constitution, or even a perpetual law. The earth belongs always to the living generation. They may manage it then, & what proceeds from it, as they please, during their usufruct. They are masters too of their own persons, & consequently may govern them as they please. But persons & property make the sum of the objects of government. The constitution and the laws of their predecessors extinguished then in their natural course, with those who gave them being. This could preserve that being till it ceased to be itself, & no longer. Every constitution then, & every law, naturally expires at the end of 19 years. If it be enforced longer, it is an act of force, & not of right. It may be said that the succeeding generation exercising in fact the power of repeal, this leaves them as free as if the constitution or law had been expressly limited to 19 years only. In the first place, this objection admits the right, in proposing an equivalent. But the power of repeal is not an equivalent. It might be indeed if every form of government were so perfectly contrived that the will of the majority could always be obtained fairly & without impediment. But this is true of no form. The people cannot assemble themselves. Their representation is unequal & vicious. Various checks are opposed to every legislative proposition. Factions get possession of the public councils. Bribery corrupts them. Personal interests lead them astray from the general interests of their constituents: and other impediments arise so as to prove to every practical man that a law of limited duration is much more manageable than one which needs a repeal.

This principle that the earth belongs to the living, & not to the dead, is of very extensive application & consequences, in every country, and most especially in France. It enters into the resolution of the questions Whether the nation may change the descent of lands holden in tail? Whether they may change the appropriation of lands given anciently to the church, to hospitals, colleges, orders of chivalry, & otherwise in perpetuity? Whether they may abolish the charges & privileges attached on lands, including the whole catalogue ecclesiastical & feudal? It goes to hereditary offices, authorities & jurisdictions; to hereditary orders, distinctions & appellations; to perpetual monopolies in commerce, the arts & sciences; with a long train of et ceteras: and it renders the question of reimbursement a question of generosity &

not of right. In all these cases, the legislature of the day could authorize such appropriations & establishments for their own time, but no longer; & the present holders, even where they, or their ancestors, have purchased, are in the case of bonâ fide purchasers of what the seller had no right to convey.

Turn this subject in your mind, my dear Sir, & particularly as to the power of contracting debts; & develop it with that perspicuity & cogent logic so peculiarly yours. Your station in the councils of our country gives you an opportunity of producing it to public consideration, of forcing it into discussion. At first blush it may be rallied, as a theoretical speculation: but examination will prove it to be solid & salutary. It would furnish matter for a fine preamble to our first law for appropriating the public revenue; & it will exclude at the threshold of our government the contagious & ruinous errors of this quarter of the globe, which have armed despots with means, not sanctioned by nature, for binding in chains their fellow men. We have already given in example one effectual check to the Dog of war, by transferring the power of letting him loose from the Executive to the Legislative body, from those who are to spend to those who are to pay. I should be pleased to see this second obstacle held out by us also in the first instance. No nation can make a declaration against the validity of long-contracted debts so disinterestedly as we, since we do not owe a shilling which may not be paid with ease, principal & interest, within the time of our own lives. Establish the principle also in the new law to be passed for protecting copyrights & new inventions, by securing the exclusive right for 19. instead of 14. years. Besides familiarizing us to this term, it will be an instance the more of our taking reason for our guide, instead of

English precedent, the habit of which fetters us with all the political heresies of a nation equally remarkable for its early excitement from some errors, and long slumbering under others.

I write you no news, because, when an occasion occurs, I shall write a separate letter for that. I am always with great & sincere esteem, dear Sir Your affectionate friend & servant,

To Peter Carr
Paris, August 10, 1787

Jefferson loved to write letters of advice to young people, particularly if he could mentor them in their educational pursuits. This one was written to his nephew Peter Carr, who eventually became something of a disappointment to Jefferson, who had no living sons. What makes this letter so remarkable is Jefferson's careful advice to his nephew about religious questions: Does God exist? Is Jesus the son of God? What happens if I decide I'm an atheist or a deist? Had this letter found its way into Federalist or evangelical hands, Jefferson would have been subjected to withering criticism. Suggesting that Carr read the Bible just as he would read any other ancient text (Tacitus or Livy) would have enraged devout Christians. Still, notice that Uncle Jefferson urged Carr not to approach these important questions with an irreverent attitude: "divest yourself of all bias in favour of novelty and singularity of opinion." In other words, this is too important a subject to play games with. Thomas Jefferson was a genuine freethinker. Just what he believed is hard to ascertain, but he could not accept the idea of the Trinity, he doubted the divinity of Jesus, and he removed the miracles and most of the healings from the New Testament he cut up for his private edification. I wish those who managed my adolescence had written me a letter of this quality and generosity of spirit.

Dear Peter

I have received your two letters of December. 30 and April 18. and am very happy to find by them, as well as by letters from Mr. Wythe, that you have been so fortunate as to attract his notice and good will: I am sure you will find this to have been one of the most fortunate events of your life, as I have ever been sensible it was of mine. I enclose you a sketch of the sciences to which I would wish you to apply in such order as Mr. Wythe shall advise; I mention also the books in them worth your reading, which submit to his correction. Many of these are among your father's books, which you should have brought to you. As I do not recollect those of them not in his library, you must write to me for them, making out a catalogue of such as you think you shall have occasion for in 18 months from the date of your letter, and consulting Mr. Wythe on the subject. To this sketch I will add a few particular observations.

1. Italian. I fear the learning this language will confound your French and Spanish. Being all of them degenerated dialects of the Latin, they are apt to mix in conversation. I have never seen a person speaking the three languages who did not mix them. It is a delightful language, but late events having rendered the Spanish more useful, lay it aside to prosecute that.

2. Spanish. Bestow great attention on this, and endeavor to acquire an accurate knowledge of it. Our future connections with Spain and Spanish America will render that language a valuable acquisition. The antient history of a great part of America too is written in that language. I send you a dictionary.

3. Moral philosophy. I think it lost time to attend lectures in this branch. He who made us would have been a pitiful

bungler if he had made the rules of our moral conduct a matter of science. For one man of science, there are thousands who are not. What would have become of them? Man was destined for society. His morality therefore was to be formed to this object. He was endowed with a sense of right and wrong merely relative to this. This sense is as much a part of his nature as the sense of hearing, seeing, feeling; it is the true foundation of morality, and not the truth, &c., as fanciful writers have imagined. The moral sense, or conscience, is as much a part of man as his leg or arm. It is given to all human beings in a stronger or weaker degree, as force of members is given them in a greater or less degree. It may be strengthened by exercise, as may any particular limb of the body. This sense is submitted indeed in some degree to the guidance of reason; but it is a small stock which is required for this: even a less one than what we call Common sense. State a moral case to a ploughman and a professor. The former will decide it as well, and often better than the latter, because he has not been led astray by artificial rules. In this branch therefore read good books because they will encourage as well as direct your feelings. The writings of Sterne particularly form the best course of morality that ever was written. Besides these read the books mentioned in the enclosed paper; and above all things lose no occasion of exercising your dispositions to be grateful, to be generous, to be charitable, to be humane, to be true, just, firm, orderly, courageous &c. Consider every act of this kind as an exercise which will strengthen your moral faculties, and increase your worth.

4. Religion. Your reason is now mature enough to receive this object. In the first place divest yourself of all bias in favor of novelty and singularity of opinion. Indulge them in any

other subject rather than that of religion. It is too important, and the consequences of error may be too serious. On the other hand shake off all the fears and servile prejudices under which weak minds are servilely crouched. Fix reason firmly in her seat, and call to her tribunal every fact, every opinion. Question with boldness even the existence of a god; because, if there be one, he must more approve the homage of reason, than that of blindfolded fear. You will naturally examine first the religion of your own country. Read the bible then, as you would read Livy or Tacitus. The facts which are within the ordinary course of nature you will believe on the authority of the writer, as you do those of the same kind in Livy and Tacitus. The testimony of the writer weighs in their favor in one scale, and their not being against the laws of nature does not weigh against them. But those facts in the bible which contradict the laws of nature, must be examined with more care, and under a variety of faces. Here you must recur to the pretensions of the writer to inspiration from god. Examine upon what evidence his pretensions are founded, and whether that evidence is so strong as that it's falsehood would be more improbable than a change of the laws of nature in the case he relates. For example in the book of Joshua we are told the sun stood still several hours. Were we to read that fact in Livy or Tacitus we should class it with their showers of blood, speaking of statues, beasts &c., but it is said that the writer of that book was inspired. Examine therefore candidly what evidence there is of his having been inspired. The pretension is entitled to your enquiry, because millions believe it. On the other hand you are Astronomer enough to know how contrary it is to the law of nature that a body revolving on its axis, as the earth does, should have stopped, should not by that sudden stoppage have prostrated animals, trees, buildings, and should after a certain time have resumed its revolution, and that without a second general prostration. Is this arrest of the earth's motion, or the evidence which affirms it, most within the law of probabilities? You will next read the new testament. It is the history of a personage called Jesus. Keep in your eye the opposite pretensions. Of those who say he was begotten by god, born of a virgin, suspended and reversed the laws of nature at will, and ascended bodily into heaven: and of those who say he was a man, of illegitimate birth, of a benevolent heart, enthusiastic mind, who set out without pretensions to divinity, ended in believing them, and was punished capitally for sedition by being gibbeted according to the Roman law which punished the first commission of that offence by whipping, and the second by exile or death in furcâ. See this law in the Digest Lib. 48. tit. 19 § 28. 3. and Lipsius Lib. 2. de cruce. cap. 2. These questions are examined in the books I have mentioned under the head of religion, and several others. They will assist you in your enquiries, but keep your reason firmly on the watch in reading them all. Do not be frightened from this enquiry by any fear of its consequences. If it ends in a belief that there is no god, you will find incitements to virtue in the comfort and pleasantness you feel in its exercise, and the love of others which it will procure you. If you find reason to believe there is a god, a consciousness that you are acting under his eye, and that he approves you, will be a vast additional incitement. If that there be a future state, the hope of a happy existence in that increases the appetite to deserve it; if that Jesus was also a god, you will be comforted by a belief of his aid and love. In fine, I repeat that you must lay aside all prejudice on both sides, and neither believe nor reject any thing because any other person, or description of persons have rejected or believed it. Your own reason is the only oracle given you by heaven, and you are answerable not for the rightness but uprightness of the decision.—I forgot to observe when speaking of the New testament that you should read all the histories of Christ, as well of those whom a council of ecclesiastics have decided for us to be Pseudo-evangelists, as those they named Evangelists, because these Pseudo-evangelists pretended to inspiration as much as the others, and you are to judge their pretensions by your own reason, and not by the reason of those ecclesiastics. Most of these are lost. There are some however still extant, collected by Fabricius which I will endeavor to get and send you.

5. Travelling. This makes men wiser, but less happy. When men of sober age travel, they gather knowledge which they may apply usefully for their country, but they are subject ever after to recollections mixed with regret, their affections are weakened by being extended over more objects, and they learn new habits which cannot be gratified when they return home. Young men who travel are exposed to all these inconveniences in a higher degree, to others still more serious, and do not acquire that wisdom for which a previous foundation is requisite by repeated and just observations at home. The glare of pomp and pleasure is analogous to the motion of their blood, it absorbs all their affection and attention, they are torn from it as from the only good in this world, and return to their home as to a place of exile and condemnation. Their eyes are forever turned back to the object they have lost, and it's recollection poisons the residue of their lives. Their first and most delicate passions are hackneyed on unworthy objects here, and they carry home only the dregs, insufficient to make themselves or anybody else happy. Add to this that a habit of idleness, an inability to apply themselves to business is acquired and renders them useless to themselves and their country. These observations are founded in experience. There is no place where your

pursuit of knowledge will be so little obstructed by foreign objects as in your own country, nor any wherein the virtues of the heart will be less exposed to be weakened. Be good, be learned, and be industrious, and you will not want the aid of travelling to render you precious to your country, dear to your friends, happy within yourself. I repeat my advice to take a great deal of exercise, and on foot. Health is the first requisite after morality. Write to me often and be assured of the interest I take in your success, as well as of the warmth of those sentiments of attachment with which I am, dear Peter, your affectionate friend,

P.S. Let me know your age in your next letter. Your cousins here are well and desire to be remembered to you.

To James Madison
Fontainebleau, October 28, 1785

The letters Jefferson wrote to his closest friend James Madison from France are remarkable for his willingness to wrestle with the fundamental issues of civilization. My view is that Jefferson was a book radical before he went to Europe in 1784, but he became a much more passionate radical when he saw the collapse of a failed state. He saw the fertility of the French countryside, noted a climate ideal for agricultural production, and admired the character of the French people, so the question was, what went wrong? In this great letter, Jefferson reflects upon a chance encounter with a French peasant. What he wanted to know was how the United States could avoid vast accumulations of wealth in the hands of the few while the many barely found it possible to put food on the table. His solution was carefully targeted redistribution—but only if necessary—so that no able-bodied person would be unable to subsist. Jefferson's solution—for which as a lover of liberty and an antagonist to intrusive government he was wary—was a geometrically graduated income tax—but only if necessary. It is not necessary for us to agree with Jefferson's solution; what matters is that he was willing to explore these very difficult questions in his letters to Madison, whom he knew would take them seriously, but who would also challenge Jefferson's views if he regarded them as illogical or impracticable.

Dear Sir

Seven o'clock, and retired to my fireside, I have determined to enter into conversation with you; this is a village of about 5,000 inhabitants when the court is not here and 20,000 when they are, occupying a valley thro' which runs a brook, and on each side of it a ridge of small mountains most of which are naked rock. The king comes here in the fall always, to hunt. His court attend him, as do also the foreign diplomatic corps. But as this is not indispensably required, and my finances do not admit the expense of a continued residence here, I propose to come occasionally to attend the king's levees, returning again to Paris, distant 40 miles. This being the first trip, I set out yesterday morning to take a view of the place. For this purpose I shaped my course towards the highest of the mountains in sight, to the top of which was about a league. As soon as I had got clear of the town I fell in with a poor woman walking at the same rate with myself and going the same course. Wishing to know the condition of the laboring poor I entered into conversation with her, which I began by enquiries for the path which would lead me into the mountain: and thence proceeded to enquiries into her vocation, condition and circumstance. She told me she was a day laborer, at 8 sous or 4d sterling the day; that she had two children to maintain, and to pay a rent of 30 livres for her house (which would consume the hire of 75 days), that often she could get no employment, and of course was without bread. As we had walked together near a mile and she had so far served me as a guide, I gave her, on parting 24 sous. She burst into tears of a gratitude which I could perceive was unfeigned, because she was unable to utter a word. She had probably never before received so great an aid. This little attendrissement, with the solitude of my walk led me into a train of reflections on that unequal division of property which occasions the numberless instances of wretchedness which I had observed in this country and is to be observed all over Europe. The property of this country is absolutely concentered in a very few hands, having revenues of from half a million of guineas a year downwards. These employ the flower of the country as servants, some of them having as many as 200 domestics, not laboring. They employ also a great number of manufacturers, and tradesmen, and lastly the class of laboring husbandmen. But after all these comes the most numerous of all the classes, that is, the poor who cannot find work. I asked myself what could be the reason that so many should be permitted to beg who are willing to work, in a country where there is a very considerable proportion of uncultivated lands? These lands are kept idle mostly for the sake of game. It should seem then that it must be because of the enormous wealth of the proprietors which places them above attention to the increase of their revenues by permitting these lands to be labored. I am conscious that an equal division of property is impracticable. But the consequences of this enormous inequality producing so much misery to the bulk of mankind, legislators cannot invent too many devices for subdividing property, only taking care to let their subdivisions go hand in hand with the natural affections of the human mind. The descent of property of every kind therefore to all the children, or to all the brothers and sisters, or other relations in equal degree is a politic measure, and a practicable one. Another means of silently lessening the inequality of property is to exempt all from taxation below a certain point, and to tax the higher portions of property in geometrical progression as they rise. Whenever there is in any country, uncultivated lands and unemployed poor, it is clear that the laws of property have been so far extended as to violate natural right. The earth is given as a common stock for man to labor and live on. If, for the encouragement of industry we allow it to be appropriated, we must take care that other employment be furnished to those excluded from the appropriation. If we do not the fundamental right to labor the earth returns to the unemployed. It is too soon yet in our country to say that every man who cannot find employment but who can find uncultivated land, shall be at liberty to cultivate it, paying a moderate rent. But it is not too soon to provide by every possible means that as few as possible shall be without a little portion of land. The small landholders are the most precious part of a state. The next object which struck my attention in my walk was the deer with which the wood abounded. They were of the kind called 'Cerfs' and are certainly of the same species with ours. They are blackish indeed under the belly, and not white as ours, and they are more of the chestnut red: but these are such small differences as would be sure to happen in two races from the same stock, breeding separately a number of ages.—Their hares are totally different from the animal we call by that name: but their rabbet is almost exactly like him. The only difference is in their manners; the land on which I walked for some time being absolutely reduced to a honeycomb by their burrowing. I think there is no instance of ours burrowing. After descending the hill again I saw a man cutting fern. I went to him under the pretense of asking the shortest road to the town, and afterwards asked for what use he was cutting fern. He told me that this part of the country furnished a great deal of fruit to Paris. That when packed in straw it acquired an ill taste, but that dry fern preserved it perfectly without communicating any taste at all. I treasured this observation for the preservation of my apples on my return to my own country. They have no apple here to compare with our Newtown pipping. They have nothing which deserves the name of a peach; there being not sun enough to ripen the plumbpeach and the best of their soft peaches being like our autumn peaches. Their cherries and strawberries are fair, but I think less flavored. Their plumbs I think are better; so also the gooseberries, and the pears infinitely beyond anything we possess. They have no grape better than our sweet water. But they have a succession of as good from very early in the summer till frost. I am tomorrow to go to Mr. Malsherbes (an uncle of the Chevalr. Luzerne's) about 7 leagues from hence, who is the most curious man in France as to his trees. He is making for me a collection of the vines from which the Burgundy, Champagne, Bordeaux, Frontignac, and other of the most valuable wines of this country are made. Another gentleman is collecting for me the best eating grapes, including what we call the raisin. I propose also to endeavor to colonize their hare, rabbet, red and grey partridge, pheasants of different kinds, and some other birds. But I find that I am wandering beyond the limits of my walk and will therefore bid you Adieu. Yours affectionately,

Acknowledgments

E
verett Albers taught me to project Jefferson into a world he did not live to see without letting my own politics or opinions distort the lens. Ev was the great executive director of the North Dakota Humanities Council, where I cut my teeth as a public humanities scholar. He invented the modern tent Chautauqua movement. He gave me the best intellectual advice I have ever received: judgment is easy, understanding is hard.

I'm indebted to my friend David Swenson of Makoche Recording Studios in Bismarck, North Dakota. David has been "the semi-permanent guest host" of the Thomas Jefferson Hour for fifteen years. People who listen to our public radio program and podcast say they can hear the friendship. That matters to me more than anything else. His son Graham Swenson has brought the Jefferson Hour into the twenty-first century.

Beth Kaylor has brought order to my work. There is nothing better than whimsical collaboration. She got this project off square one, for which I am immensely grateful. She manages the Jefferson Hour cultural tours with rigor and élan. Nancy Franke has been my scheduler and handler for a long time now. She has made it possible for me to give my best energies to reading, writing, speaking, and cogitating.

Ann Lucas, Jack Robertson, and Pat Brodowski of Thomas Jefferson's Monticello have thrown open the garden gate and the magical parlor doors of Monticello to me. Thanks to Pat I have put my hands into the soil of Jefferson's fabulous garden, and thanks to Ann I have had the chance to lecture in Jefferson's "Indian Hall" at Monticello and lead Monticello's friends up the dreaded Wendover Mountain Hike on the Lewis and Clark Trail.

Without Mike Jacobs I would never have become a writer or a naturalized North Dakotan. He (and the *Grand Forks Herald*) won the Pulitzer Prize for their heroic coverage of the 1997 Red River Flood in Grand Forks, North Dakota.

America's greatest documentary filmmaker Ken Burns has given me the opportunity to provide what insights I can in five of his films, the first of them his 1998 study of Jefferson.

Prairie Public Radio in North Dakota, High Plains Public Radio in Kansas and the Texas Panhandle, and WHRO in Norfolk have been my flagship stations, and Salida, Colorado, is where Jefferson would live if he were really an anarchist.

Levi Bachmeier of West Fargo, North Dakota, is the future of a state that Eric Sevareid, who grew up here, called "a large rectangular blank spot in the nation's mind." He has helped me understand a state I have lived in three times as long as he has been alive.

My editor, Joe Coccaro, made this a much better book.

My daughter, Catherine, who is an occasional host of the Jefferson Hour, exemplifies everything that I prize in life.

CPSIA information can be obtained
at www.ICGtesting.com
Printed in the USA
BVHW030201100820
585946BV00001B/70

9 781646 630967